Why Girls Fight

Why Girls Fight

Female Youth Violence in the Inner City

Cindy D. Ness

NEW YORK UNIVERSITY PRESS
New York and London

NEW YORK UNIVERSITY PRESS
New York and London
www.nyupress.org

Library of Congress Cataloging-in-Publication Data

Ness, Cindy D., 1959–
Why girls fight : female youth violence in the inner city / Cindy D. Ness.
p. cm.
Includes bibliographical references and index.
ISBN-13: 978–0–8147–5840–3 (cl : alk. paper)
ISBN-10: 0–8147–5840–1 (cl : alk. paper)
ISBN-13: 978–0–8147–5841–0 (pb : alk. paper)
ISBN-10: 0–8147–5841–x (pb : alk. paper)
[etc.]
1. Female juvenile delinquents—United States.
2. Teenage girls—Psychology. 3. Inner cities—United States.
4. Minorities—United States—Psychology. I. Title.
HV6791.N38   2010
303.60835'20973—dc22   2009053831

New York University Press books are printed on acid-free paper,
and their binding materials are chosen for strength and durability.
We strive to use environmentally responsible suppliers and materials
to the greatest extent possible in publishing our books.

Manufactured in the United States of America

c 10 9 8 7 6 5 4 3 2 1
p 10 9 8 7 6 5 4 3 2 1

To Alden, who makes it special every day

Contents

Preface

The actual time it takes to write a book, though lengthy, is far shorter than the time it takes to become the person who writes that book. What follows is the result of a long period of intellectual meandering come to its natural resting point.

During the late 1980s and early 1990s, as a newly minted social worker in New York City teaching hospitals and mental health agencies, it did not take long for me to grow disenchanted with the disciplinary paradigms meant to explain why minority youths in economically impoverished urban neighborhoods so readily engaged in violence, nor did it take me long to grow extremely skeptical of the institutions charged with "fixing" them. It became clear in talking day after day and, eventually, year after year with "these" kids that something larger than their personal foibles was driving the curiously consistent demographics of referrals to day-treatment programs, diagnostic facilities, and the juvenile justice system. It also became clear to me that violence by inner-city youths was not simply a dysfunctional compensatory adaptation to frustration or, worse yet, unbridled sociopathy, as it mostly was portrayed to be. Searching for a sensible way to think dynamically about social organization, culture, and the psychological development of children and adolescents in American inner-city neighborhoods, rather than continuing to consider them the separate "bounded" entities of inquiry that the social sciences of the time made them out to be, led me to travel for a while (literally) in different directions.

In the mid 1990s I found my way to the Center on Violence and Human Survival at CUNY's John Jay College of Criminal Justice, where I subsequently spent nearly a decade working either directly with Robert Jay Lifton or in close proximity to his work. Lifton's way of delving into issues of mass violence offered me my entry point to think about the intersection of violence, cultural influences, and individual psychology, though I would ultimately focus on the practice and structure of violence in urban settings myself. Our conversations about large-scale violent events were extremely valuable to the development of my ideas about how a social and cultural phenomenon becomes a psychological one.

In 1997, while maintaining a clinical psychotherapy practice in New York City and serving as Lifton's research assistant for the book he was writing on the Japanese cult Aum Shinrikyo, I began doctoral study at Harvard University with Carol Gilligan, whom I had met at Lifton's annual Wellfleet seminar the year before. I was particularly interested in Gilligan's qualitative approach to narrative based on relational psychological theory. In Gilligan's method, the act of listening is structured to open a window into the associative logic of a person's inner world—ordinarily the territory of a clinical interview—at the same time that the listener considers the larger influences of context in a person's narrative. As identity arises out of messages about the "self" received from all quarters, I wanted to find a way to take into account those emanating from a person's social world: essentially, to listen to how the emotional logic of a given individual and the logic of a given cultural setting come together.

While at Harvard, I also spent hours in conversation with anthropologist Robert LeVine concerning the work of Edward Sapir—a first-generation student of Franz Boas, who was a leading voice in the culture and personality movement of the 1920s and 1930s and an interdisciplinary thinker par excellence. Sapir was bent on making sense of how patterns in the cultural order were individually adapted by people and made their own. Sapir drew attention to the fact that psychiatry did not typically credit culture with the ability to modify "the actual persisting personality" and its "private symbolisms": rather personality was viewed as overriding or overruling culture. Sapir argued that the variation that existed within any given culture was sufficient to override all cultural forces, even the most subtle ones. It was the social scientist's task to make sense of the pushes and pulls that influence behavior, not subdivide them into discrete components or simply sort them into countable categories.

In 2000, given what I, too, came to perceive to be the inextricability of culture and personality, I set off to pursue a second doctorate, in anthropology, at the University of Pennsylvania. There I engaged in ongoing discussion with sociologist Elijah Anderson, which provided yet another essential piece of the intellectual framework that I would bring to my work. Anderson had written extensively on the use of violence by males in American inner cities and of the informal "code of the street" that placed a premium on respect. My interest was to adapt Anderson's work to the use of physical violence by female youths in inner cities, including a consideration of the girls' emotional lives. Armed with the canon of three disciplines, I felt I was almost ready to try to answer the question: Why do girls in inner cities fight?

As I got deeper into the research that led to this book, however, I became acutely aware of the increased participation of women in violence around the globe, whether in ethno-separatist struggles where they had come to make up 30% to 40% of combatants, as suicide bombers, or as perpetrators of violent criminal offenses, and I found myself wondering what it meant. The curiosity let loose in me resulted in somewhat of a detour, though the timing was not wholly whimsical. After Lifton retired from CUNY, I continued on staff at the Center on Terrorism under the directorship of Chuck Strozier, with whom I had also worked closely for many years at the Center on Violence and Human Survival. It resulted in my guest editing an issue of the journal *Studies in Conflict and Terrorism*, focused on women; editing a book on the subject, titled *Female Terrorism and Militancy: Agency, Organization, and Utility*; and publishing an article in *Daedelus*, titled "The Rise of Female Violence." What became quite clear was that wherever the use of violence by women was found, no matter how widely disparate the cultural realities were that surrounded it, a careful analysis of the interplay of macro and micro forces was needed to fully explain it.

Appreciating that norms regarding the use of violence by females had undergone a marked shift (not only in conflict zones where the need to defend one's life or rights is acute but also in Western mainstream culture) has been important to the writing of this book, though in not fully realized ways. Interestingly, around the same time that violent arrest rates for female youths began to increase in the United States, violent females came to be lauded in American media not as gender anomalies but as both worthy allies in a physical confrontation and formidable opponents in their own right. Our movies and television programs came to tell us daily that violence had ceased to reside wholly in the hands of boys and men. They also suggested that female-perpetrated violence was no longer the province of disenfranchised neighborhoods where the living was hard. No doubt, this democratization of violence on the screen took our cultural imagination about the capacity of females to embrace physical aggression beyond the confines where it once was held, but to what effect?

While not pretending to understand the larger meaning of this trend, I would argue that, perhaps, in some small way, it gave us permission as researchers in the social sciences to conceive of violence with respect to gender more freely and, therefore, ultimately, more scientifically. I believe it made the violence I witnessed at the hands of girls in West and North Philadelphia seem less of an "unnatural" phenomenon, in that it was both in its most negative and "glamorized" extremes the stuff of prime-time TV. Certainly, residents of the neighborhoods I spoke with have known for a long time that not only are females the victims of violence, but they can also mete out violence for a range of reasons. They have lived violence not as the gendered phenomenon it has often been made out to be but in ways that make sense in the context of their life circumstances. In essence, then, this book is an attempt to add to the literature on girls' violence a depiction of a reality they are well familiar with.

Around 2000, when I first began thinking about girls' fighting, there were few if any ethnographies on the subject. That has not changed much as I complete this book, though the subject has received a windfall of valuable attention compared with what it had previously known. In an effort to begin to address the knowledge gap surrounding the use of "ordinary" violence or street fighting by girls (with which school, mental health, and police personnel deal on a daily basis), in this book I address how the institutional infrastructure, culture, and socioeconomic realities in two Philadelphia neighborhoods loosely mediate girls' fighting. In general, I tried to understand how the ethos of the neighborhoods as related to violence—its norms, values, and practices—was individually and collectively appropriated. Although such a schema does not map into an exact formula for predicting individual behavior, as individuals always exercise unique agency, this book aims to highlight the interdependence and mutual influence of the three levels of psychology, culture, and institutional structures on the use of violence by girls.

This said, it is not lost on me that the project of rendering a snapshot of human emotion and behavior, the flow of culture, and the effects of institutions accurately as they meld to produce behavior is a tall order and—in all honesty—perhaps an impossible one, although I could not have written this book if I did not believe there was some merit in trying to capture something of it. To this point, some words of Edward Zigler, the father of Head Start in this country, have stuck in my head and have given me comfort, though I suspect I have appropriated them in a way he did not intend. Zigler gave a talk at a conference pertaining to child development and effective education programs, which I attended some 15 years ago. This man, who has dedicated his life to developing an evidence-based approach to formulating sound child-development policy, told his audience that, while we do not know everything we need to know about providing children with an adequate foundation to maximize their potential, we do know enough to do far more than what we are doing. Hence, it is not perfect knowledge that we must have at our disposal to improve the life chances of children in poor enclaves, but extensive knowledge—a distinction that makes the conduct of "doing social science" a more realistic endeavor, to my mind. Zigler went on to forcefully argue that it is finding the political will to put into play what we do know that is crucial in the end.

Ultimately, I think most folks doing research on vulnerable youths understand that the crafting of sensible and compassionate public policies to address root causes, along with legislation that turns them into state and federal law, is fundamental to realizing a "good-enough" early playing field for all of America's children. Recently, I have come to witness first-hand the political gauntlet that well-documented social science research must traverse and how such research still does not often factor into policy decisions. I would strongly argue that addressing this disconnect needs to be made a bigger part of social science's mission to keep itself relevant. I have much respect for the arduous work of those who advocate for child welfare reform, though I am only just beginning to appreciate the complexities of what that entails.

In sum, the ten-year journey that accompanied the writing of this book was at times a lonely one and, at some points, an unnecessarily long one, though I am not sure I could have undertaken it differently. In what may be my only act of economy, I have genuinely thanked the people who needed to be thanked along the way. Yet while I have thanked her before, especially each time a publication deadline came and went, I would like to here offer special thanks to my editor, Jennifer Hammer. This is a woman who possesses the virtue of patience. Her unwavering wise counsel has no doubt made this book a better one in the end, for which I am grateful.

My hope is that this book will bring a more-dimensional and more-compassionate visibility to female youth who engage in violence and their families. To my eyes, the girls in the pages that follow, while often exceedingly harsh in their words and actions, are very much children.

Introduction

If I seem like I'm scared to fight, some girl is gonna think she can mess with me all the time. I mean, even if I don't seem scared, she's gonna try me at some point till she knows how I am. She just better not go crying to anyone that I beat her the fuck up. I hate it when someone is a sore loser.

—Tamika, a 15-year-old girl

Fighting is about image. It's about showing you're no punk. I know I don't rule the world, but I can feel like I do, make you think I do. Fighting is independence. I beat someone up if I feel like it.

—Allie, a 14-year-old girl

You kidding me, girls be fighting more than boys do. They so emotional they'll fight over anything. Boys won't get into it over no he-said, she-said. They only gonna fight over something serious like money or drugs. That's not what a girl is fighting about most of the time.

—Kia, a 15-year-old girl

On any given day in the West and Northeast Philadelphia neighborhoods that I refer to as Melrose Park and Lee, respectively, it is not uncommon to hear about a street fight that has "gone down" between girls. In certain instances, the fight takes place in a school hallway; in others, after the school day ends at a given time and place. Or perhaps it breaks out spontaneously on a street corner or a park after one girl provokes another past the point where she either must "step up" to a situation or otherwise be labeled a "punk." Far less common, though certainly not unheard of, is a scenario in which a female youth challenges a male youth to a fight or is likewise challenged to one. However, in any of these cases, whether she wins or loses, it is standing up to the challenge more than anything else that earns a girl a sense of respect among her peers. While much has been written about the relationship between violence and respect as it applies to male youths in low-income neighborhoods, the literature is virtually silent along these lines concerning girls.[1]

Why do female adolescent youths in impoverished urban neighborhoods so readily engage in street fights and other forms of physical violence? The answer is far more complicated than the dichotomous morality tale of girls who are "good" and girls who are "bad," the explanation that the use of physical aggression by girls has historically been accorded. Indeed, rather than being characteristic of only a relatively small subset of female youths with social and emotional problems who are prone to delinquency, street fighting is an important part of girlhood in high-crime neighborhoods. In such neighborhoods, physical aggression becomes an acceptable and normative, albeit regrettable, response for girls and sometimes even for the mothers of girls if their daughters are outnumbered in a fight or if a fight is brought to the household doorstep.

The vignette that follows describes an actual fight that took place in Melrose Park over a period of several days in which two girls, their mothers, female peers, and female relatives all got involved. As with most fights, the subtlest body movements and verbal barbs send a message about how ready one is to cross the line into physical violence. The participants, who all know each other, are "experienced observers" in the neighborhood, with respect to what constitutes a challenge that can be walked away from as opposed to one that must be met head on. While the encounter is at first characterized by verbal attack and posturing, and it seems like the girls have no intention of actually fighting, the demeanor and displays of ego are just a first step in the buildup to an actual and larger altercation that transpires days later. The issue at hand is perceived to be important enough to bring family members into the fray, as well as neighbors if necessary.

Marcea comes walking down the block with her girlfriends and sees her boyfriend Rashid sitting between two girls, Lakeesha and Candace, on a stoop. Marcea is clearly incensed over Rashid's proximity to Candace. She demands that Rashid come over to her, and Lakeesha and Candace erupt in laughter. Marcea is making a scene in the middle of the street but without approaching. It is Candace who is first to goad her to say something directly. In return, Marcea's friends egg her on, and within seconds she is cursing in Candace's face. Candace stands up, and the girls challenge each other to fight. Though verbal insults and pointed fingers are flying, with the other girls holding shoes and handbags and pulling the two apart at critical moments, it is truly amazing that Marcea and Candace do not actually touch. In the midst of the chaos, Rashid has disappeared. After a good five minutes of posturing, each girl labels the other a punk and the two groups disperse. But it is clear that the situation is not resolved. The question is when and where it will erupt next.

About an hour later, Marcea's mother and seven or eight females come to Candace's sister's house, where Candace lives. The older women hanging out on Candace's block stand within striking distance should they be needed. Marcea's mother and Candace's sister exchange words, and at one point Marcea's mother yells, "just because I have my keefah [religious garb] on, don't think I can't get ignorant with you." She makes it clear that Rashid is like her son and that Candace needs to stay away from him. Candace's sister, however, no longer wants to discuss this incident. She confronts Marcea's mother about bringing the situation to her doorstep. Both women clearly lay out which boundaries cannot be crossed. This seems to be enough to end the matter for the evening.

Two days later, Lakeesha beats up Marcea because "she said stupid things, so I punched her in her face." While Candace will fight to save face, hence all the showmanship, Lakeesha has historically had more of a proclivity toward fighting, although much less so recently. Already angry about something else, she took care of the situation for Candace. However, the situation was more complex than Lakeesha happening on an opportunity to let off some steam. Marcea had continued to talk badly about Candace in public and threatened to beat Candace up at some later time. There was an understanding between Candace and Lakeesha that if either needed help in managing a physical confrontation, the other would step in. As such, Lakeesha perceived the bad-mouthing of Candace to be a show of disrespect to her, as well. To let the situation go on for much longer would be a blemish on the reputation she had made for herself as a girl with "heart" and not one who is a patsy.

Although they all live in the same community within two blocks from each other, Lakeesha and Candace, Marcea's mother, and Candace's sister and guardian each have a different relationship to violence, the explanation for which can be found in the details of their personal stories. While each is aware of the set of shared meanings or "understandings," social rules, and relationship terms that surround the resort to physical aggression by girls in their neighborhood, each has come to appropriate these understandings differently. At the same time, it would be impossible to explain the fighting sequence described above without also crediting the influence that larger macro factors and organizational structures have on the identity, perceptions, and values of girls and women living in Melrose Park and Lee.

Historically, however, the social sciences have dealt with macro-level and individual-level factors as separate matters of inquiry, despite the fact that both levels are inextricably linked in their effects on human experience. While the trend toward connecting levels of analysis in the social sciences has become increasingly common in recent years, scholarship on girls' violence along these lines still remains relatively scant. To address this gap, in this book I explore the social and cultural organization of female youth violence in inner-city neighborhoods on a collective level, as well as the individual-level responses to those structuring conditions. I engage in an analysis and synthesis of both the macro and micro elements that inhere in a violent act—that is, its social, cultural, and psychological components.

It is essential to begin any discussion of female youth violence by first observing that the term "violent girls" is in and of itself highly problematic.[2] The assumptions that underlie the contemporary use of the term, for all intents and purposes, conform to the sociocultural ideals of white, middle-class communities. In white, middle-class communities, females are normatively conceptualized either as victims or, more recently, as perpetrating what is referred to as "relational violence": a subtle form of verbal aggression that uses relationships to manipulate and psychologically harm others. No conceptual framework exists in such communities with which to think about physically violent girls without marginalizing or devaluing them. Any girl who engages in physical violence can only be considered anomalous in terms of gender identity. In middle-class neighborhoods, such a girl is typically unpopular, except with others like herself, and is viewed by adults as being "troubled."

The term "violent girls" applied to girls in inner cities imposes a set of assumptions about proper behavior and roles, which do not correspond to the lived social realities of these girls, like the ones that I followed over a period of nearly two years: for example, that males are protectors, that females are not violent, and that females who fight are not considered feminine. The term "violent girls" does not convey that gender socialization in Melrose Park and Lee emphasizes the importance of a girl being able to defend herself. For the most part, the discourse on girls' violence centers on girls being out of control and dangerous. It does not take into consideration that girls in inner cities commonly feel they have no choice but to respond aggressively and that, by doing so, among other things, they believe themselves to be gaining a modicum of security. Unfortunately, the contribution of context has received short shrift when considering why girls turn to violence.[3]

Importantly, distinctions in race and class, which influence the profoundly different relationships that a girl can have to physical violence, tend to be implied when the subject of girls' violence is addressed in the media or the academic literature on the subject but are not typically developed in a way that meaningfully shows this interdependency. The usual takeaway message in the media is that female youth violence is mostly a minority phenomenon limited to delinquent or sociopathic girls. Few studies have systematically considered the instrumental value that engaging in violence has for girls or the normative social symbolic code that supports it in low-income minority neighborhoods.[4]

Research in the social sciences, particularly within criminology, the discipline that has taken the greatest interest in girls' violence, has almost exclusively concentrated on the most "extreme" manifestations of female youth violence and on female youth violence committed in connection with illegal activities—for example, girls who belong to gangs,[5] commit homicide,[6] are involved in drug-related violence,[7] or embrace violence as a strategy to stave off domestic victimization[8]—not the majority of instances in which girls in inner cities physically aggress.[9] Indeed, the typical display of violence by girls in inner cities is the everyday street fight, which often flies below the radar screen of accountability (i.e., is not reported to the police and does not result in arrest or emergency room visits). Though most of the violence in which females engage does not reach the level of danger to which male youth violence rises, female youth violence possesses a sophisticated organization and discourse of its own that is rooted in the social fabric of a neighborhood, its "codes," and its structures of belief.[10] If we are to adequately investigate what it means for girls in inner cities to commit physical aggression, we must take a less-narrow view of the subject and contextualize their aggression far more fully than we have yet done. In this book, I attempt to do just that.

I spent almost two years "hanging out" with girls in Melrose Park and Lee, two impoverished urban neighborhoods, observing and interviewing

them about the meanings they ascribed to their own violence. I was interested in knowing more about how girls, themselves, thought about fighting. Indeed, I wanted to know how prevalent fighting by girls really is.
I hoped to get underneath the sensationalistic accounts that dominated
the increased media coverage over the past several decades, beginning in
the mid 1970s, and see what I could discover. I wanted to get to the level
of detail that rarely reaches us about why girls in some neighborhoods
are more likely to physically aggress. Through presenting the accounts
of 16 female adolescent youths who engage in violence—in addition to
the accounts of their friends, family members, neighborhood residents,
teachers, school administrators, criminal justice professionals, and mental health personnel with whom I sought contact in order to better understand the girls' behavior—here I attempt to provide a sense of the many
complex reasons that contemporary female youths living in inner cities
resort to street fighting or other forms of violence. Though this one volume could not possibly represent the experiences of all inner-city females
who have committed or will commit violence, my hope is that it will open
the gate to more accounts expressed by girls themselves and that it will
serve to bring added dimension to the subject in the literature.

The Wider Context

In the mid 1980s, the juvenile violent crime rate in the United States
began a steep ascent, which lasted nearly a decade before peaking in 1994.
The spike, largely a phenomenon of inner-city neighborhoods, was all the
more startling because it came at a time when crime rates had been falling and were expected to continue to fall as the country's baby-boomer
population aged out of its most crime-prone years. Experts from a variety
of disciplines advanced a clash of theories to account for the surge, ranging from the moral decay of the nation's youth (in particular, DiIulio 1995,
1996) to the institutional decay of its cities. If consensus lay anywhere, it
was in identifying the crack epidemic that was well under way by the mid
1980s, and the influx of handguns that accompanied it, as the "epidemic's"
proximal causes (Blumstein and Wallman, 2000). The trend was further
exacerbated by a dramatic increase in the access to guns by juveniles.[11]
    One of the inadvertent consequences of what became known as the war
on drugs and subsequently the war on violence was the unprecedented
attention it brought to female juvenile violence. Zero-tolerance policies of

the 1990s largely put an end to the paternalism of the criminal justice system toward female criminals and resulted in many more women and girls, disproportionately poor minorities, being arrested and prosecuted.[12] The media, seizing on accounts of minority female adolescents gratuitously victimizing other youths, provided the issue with a disturbing public face that aroused fear.[13] The phrase "girls gone wild," used both by female adolescents to represent their own aggressive behavior and by the authorities in their lives—though with vastly different connotations—came to signify the essence of the phenomenon for many.

In academia, debate took shape over whether the quality and proportional quantity of girls' violence had actually changed or whether the appearance that it had was an artifact of sentencing practices and media sensationalism. Whichever the case, the use of violence by female adolescents for the first time was granted categorical significance in its own right. Though alarm bells had been sounded intermittently over the course of American history, warning of female youths engaging in increasing levels of delinquency, for the most part, the behaviors precipitating those public outcries were so-called sexual improprieties or offenses such as disorderly conduct, shoplifting, forgery, and larceny, not person crimes involving violence.[14]

Though these earlier infractions raised anxiety about moral slippage, they did not cast female juveniles as an imminent threat to society.[15] By the mid 1990s, however, the percentage rise of female juvenile violence stood out in high relief against the statistics on record for girls. Existing theories, most of which portrayed girls as being averse by nature to inflicting harm, could no longer even keep up the appearance of being sound and begged for observers to reconsider girls in relation to violence in a more-complex way and essentially anew.[16]

Although arrest rates for both male and female juvenile violent crime markedly declined after the mid 1990s, the far smaller decrease in female violence subsumed within this larger trend especially needed explanation. For example, longitudinal data revealed that the incidence of female juvenile violence had increased annually as a percentage of the total violent crime index since 1987; said another way, though the violent crime rate had decreased for all groups, the proportion of violent crime by females in relation to boys actually continued to increase. According to the Office of Juvenile Justice and Delinquency Prevention (OJJDP), the total arrest rate for girls in 2001 (112 per 100,000) was 59% above its 1980 rate (70 per 100,000), while the 2001 rate for boys (471 per 100,000) was 20% below its 1980 rate; girls accounted for 23% of juvenile arrests for aggravated assault nationwide, 32% of simple assaults, and 18% of the total violent crime index in 2001.[17] Stated from another angle, the arrest rate for simple assaults in 2003 was more than triple the amount (483.3 per 100,000) of the arrest rate for simple assaults by girls in 1980 (129.7 per 100,000) (Zahn et al., 2008). While these figures suggest that girls' violence had come into its own "statistically," the collective sociocultural processes embedded in these trend lines were poorly understood.[18] What was clear was that the incidence of physical aggression captured in these figures challenged the notion that girls were anathema to committing violence in kind. The numbers could no longer be seen as characterizing a relatively few girls who had lost their way.

I do not seek here to join the debate over whether the increased number of girls arrested for violent offenses in America today represents a genuine shift in the psyche of female youth toward violence or is the artifact of stricter sentencing laws;[19] historically, the consideration of females who engage in crime has gotten bogged down in just this kind of preoccupation. Rather, I set out to explore how female adolescents in two low-income Philadelphia neighborhoods experience inflicting physical harm and the meanings they assign to doing so. I seek to consider the instrumental and symbolic value that physical aggression, particularly street fighting, has for girls in inner cities, topics that have mostly been explored in various literatures pertaining to males (Anderson, 1999; Devine, 1996; Gilligan, 1996) but, as touched on above, have not yet systematically been examined in relation to females. I attempt to make the case that establishing a "reputation" through violence—the focus here being on street fighting—offers girls in inner cities not only a measure of physical security but also an avenue for attaining a sense of mastery, status, and self-esteem in a social setting where legal opportunities for achievement and other psychic rewards are not otherwise easily available. When girls who engage in violence are simply labeled "delinquent," these identity-confirming functions go unnoticed. I contend that, rather than simply being a "telltale" sign of individual emotional pathology, street fighting in poor urban enclaves is something that girls are expected to show themselves to be good at; indeed, in these contexts, street fighting is part of carrying out girlhood. In essence, in this volume I represent the street fighting and serious violence committed by girls on its own terms rather than as a move away from the feminine toward the masculine. This is not to say that when girls commit violence their motivations and behavior bear no likeness to those of boys who commit violence; indeed, girls' resort to violence has a sociocultural organization and symbolic framework of its own. Moreover, I present the motivations and experiences of girls involved in the criminal justice system directly in their own words. In so doing, I hope to extend the reach of their words much beyond the exposure these girls have received up to now.

In this book, I specifically investigate the use of physical aggression by poor and working-class urban girls because of the greater prerogative their neighborhoods afford females with respect to physical aggression. The more-frequent resort to violence by girls in inner cities challenges the myth that all girls are innately passive and nurturing and, in effect, opens up a wider analytical space for inquiry, not only about why inner-city girls so readily engage in violence but also why middle-class girls so readily reject it. Clearly, a girl does not invent her theory of aggression out of whole cloth but, rather, in relation to the world around her.[20] She understands the place that violence and other strategies of resistance have in her neighborhood, though individual experience translates this understanding differentially.

Conversely, it is not sufficient to simply locate patterns in culture or in terms of social organization, as there is no "one" story of female youth violence in inner cities. Rather, the inclination for girls in low-income urban settings (and elsewhere) to engage in physical aggression exists on a continuum of frequency and intensity and is mitigated by individual life circumstances. Thus, this study is conceptualized within a psychological framework and also sets out to account for the role that collective social and cultural forces play in institutionalizing girls' violence. A dual lens of analysis affords the possibility of considering how individual girls in inner cities go about making larger patterns in the cultural order their own. It is the interface between human development, culture, and institutional structures—an interface often overlooked or unrecognized—that I attempt to spell out in this volume and that I believe offers the most promise for revealing the dynamics that underwrite violence.

Ultimately, I contend that different cultural standards and social realities associated with race and class, and not simply biology and individual psychology, structure the relationship that females have to physical aggression. While an adolescent girl's concern with "reputation" and her status relative to other girls is in no way limited to inner cities, the manifestation of these concerns in physical aggression to a large extent is. I argue that the incentive/disincentive structure that normally inhibits aggression in middle-class girls does not operate similarly to inhibit violence among girls in inner cities; with few prospects in the legal economy, the consequence to a girl's future for running afoul of the law, and, in turn, the disincentive to abstain from doing so, is far less formidable in inner cities than in middle-class neighborhoods. What determines whether violent behavior will become manifest, among either males or females, is highly related to how prepared one's immediate surroundings are to supporting its expression. For instance, from a young age, rather than being positively reinforced for demonstrating passivity, inner-city girls are socialized to stand up to anyone who disrespects them and to "hold their own." Moreover, unlike their middle-class counterparts, low-income urban girls who engage in violence are not viewed as defying feminine norms; femininity as constructed by mainstream culture, while not rejected outright by low-income urban girls, is selectively appropriated alongside values that more closely fit their lives.

It is noteworthy that while these girls challenge what had been longtime well-accepted theories in the literature on female psychological development and aggression (Freud, 1933; Pollak, 1950; Feshbach, 1969; Whiting and Edwards, 1973; Maccoby and Jacklin, 1974; Hall, 1978), and to a varying extent, more recent theories, as well, it is no news to inhabitants of inner-city communities that females readily resort to violence.[21] Given the exigencies of poverty and racial oppression, African American families, in particular, have historically attempted to raise girls to be assertive and self-reliant—with respect both to speaking their minds and, when necessary, standing up for themselves physically.

African American mothers are all too aware of the strength their daughters will need to "stand their ground" and protect their families on a number of fronts: against the racial antipathy and active discrimination that mainstream society entertains against them, the systemic institutional problems that create havoc in their lives, and the readiness of individuals to use force to resolve disputes and command respect.[22] Though "assertive" plus "self-reliant" need not mean "violent," it can very well reach that end point if judged necessary. The argument in the literature that girls gravitate to violence in order to cast off patriarchy and gender inequality does not typically resonate with African American mothers. More to the point for mothers is the reality that girls and women must display physical force themselves because men are often not around to do so.[23]

Thinking through the implications of macro factors on the lives of girls must include a thorough consideration of how these factors are integrated into their psychological life. However, whereas in the last decade, the discipline of psychology has brought focused attention to the use of social or relational aggression by girls (Leadbeater and Way, 1996; Jack, 1999; Simmons, 2002; Underwood, 2003; Chesney-Lind and Irwin, 2007), it has considered physical aggression to a far lesser extent.[24] Although studies in sociology and in criminology have taken up the use of physical force by female youths more frequently, neither has addressed the psychological component of a girl's aggressing in any appreciable way. To help bridge the gap, in this book I specifically consider adolescent girls who commit physical violence, by applying an interdisciplinary lens onto how psychological and sociocultural factors interact to produce violence. I look primarily at the research method of ethnography to pursue this inquiry.

Unlike other methods of inquiry, ethnography requires a researcher to immerse himself or herself in another person's social world; in so doing, it affords an extraordinary opportunity to witness phenomena on both a collective and an individual level. The observation of variation that ethnography as a method can accommodate permits a researcher to highlight a range of reactions and competing outcomes and does not force him or her to promulgate the existence of only one local view, one set of inferred meanings and emotions, or a coherence of response that defies intuition (Ness, 2004). Although empirical studies of girls' violence can propose theories about the relationships among variables, they alone cannot capture the texture of everyday life that functions in myriad ways to shape violent behavior.[25]

It is noteworthy, however, that, despite its potential for revealing how collective meanings are held and individually revised, ethnography is seldom used this way. Most inquiries do not account for how social meanings are collectively understood by groups, while at the same time portraying the idiosyncrasies of the individual inner states of members of those groups.[26] By using an ethnographic approach, an observer is able to render a more-complex view of the multiple meanings that resorting to violence has for girls, show those meanings to be in a greater state of flux, and, ultimately, form a less-caricatured view of the effect of social and cultural forces in a single social setting (Ness, 2004). It is through combining both levels of analysis—the collective and the individual—that we are able to achieve deeper insights into urban violence.

Studying Girls' Violence

In briefly discussing how girls' violence has been studied to date, my intention is not to systematically chronicle what has come before but to selectively underscore some of the many conceptual problems that have plagued the field, particularly with respect to inner cities. As noted, there are significant holes in our understanding of the specific ways in which female adolescents in inner cities both individually and collectively nego-tiate the practice of violence. Again, while seemingly countless studies have been undertaken to shed light on various aspects of the male com-ponent of the statistics noted above, relatively few studies incorporated girls as subjects until the late 1980s, and even fewer have been exclusively devoted to them.

Of particular concern to this study is how female adolescent violence is made socially meaningful in impoverished urban neighborhoods and the process by which it achieves moral legitimacy (Ness, 2004). Whereas highly prescribed roles, norms, and expectations against aggression typically structure female behavior and social relations in middle-class neighborhoods (Simmons, 2002; Wiseman, 2002), the social and cul-tural capital (Bourdieu, 1977) of a female with a reputation for violence paradoxically increases in blighted urban neighborhoods where necessity places great premium on women being "strong." Alternatively stated, the social conditions of most inner cities reinforce the utility of girls "per-forming" violence in everyday life (Jones, 2004).

Historically, explanations in the literature concerning girls who engage in physical violence have historically centered on maladjustment. Freud's characterization of normal female psychological development as the relinquishing of active instinctual aims and the acceptance of passive ones (1925, 1931, 1933) cast female delinquency and the use of violence for most of the 20th century as a move from the feminine to the masculine. This formula, which served as the premise for many subsequent theories concerning normative and pathological gender development (Konopka, 1966, 1976; Vedder and Somerville, 1973; Campbell, 1987; Armistead et al., 1992), emphasized inner psychic structure and conflicts rather than social and cultural processes in shaping behavior (for an expanded discussion, see Ness, 2004). With certain exceptions, the normative view of female aggression through to the 1980s could be reduced to a single proposition: females normatively internalize aggression, while males externalize it

(Feshbach, 1969; Whiting and Edwards, 1973; Maccoby and Jacklin, 1974; Hall, 1978).

Even though females who committed violence were no longer characterized in terms of being sexually anomalous, violent behavior for male and female juveniles continued to be assigned different causal factors—whether a reflection of the belief that females were naturally aversive to inflicting harm and were socialized to that aversion (Block, 1984; Campbell, 1984, 1993; Steffensmeier and Allan, 1996), that they inflicted harm in small number only in imitation of male behavior (Adler and Simon, 1979; Figueria-McDonough, 1992; Rhodes and Fischer, 1993), or that this was a corrective in bringing needed attention to specific social, cultural, and economic circumstances associated with gender (Heidensohn, 1985; Chilton and Datesman, 1987; Chesney-Lind, 1989, 1997; Gilfus, 1992; Belknap, 1996; Daly and Maher, 1998). Despite their different premises, each of these accounts presented a view of females that offered no insight into their potential as active agents of aggression; in some sense, each suggested that female resort to violence was only an imitation of male behavior or a manifestation of self-defense and negated the element of aggression in their violence. It was only in the late 1980s that a handful of feminist authors, in both psychology and criminology, began to question how social forces and cultural factors were involved in producing gender differences associated with violence that were presumed to be natural (Chesney-Lind, 1989, 1992, 1997; Belknap, 1996; Daly and Maher, 1998).[27] This scholarship played a major role in broadening and deepening the discourse on girls' violence and led to its development as a recognized area of inquiry.

While some research—mostly on gangs—has been undertaken to consider what function violence serves for adolescent girls—for example, as a source of protection and monetary gain (Campbell, 1984; Brotherton, 1996; Miller, 2001)—such work remains the exception and does not amount to a corpus large enough to sufficiently illuminate the issues material to the subject. Indeed, female adolescents who engage in violence are still rarely depicted as rational actors, whereas the use of physical aggression by adolescent boys is typically depicted in terms of its instrumental value in the literature—that is, violence serving a strategic purpose; its use by adolescent girls is more typically depicted as being "expressive," as a way of decreasing emotional tension that gets triggered by perceived insults or trivial arguments. Few if any studies have illuminated the ways in which issues of race and class are also central to informing the instrumental value and symbolic meaning that violence has for girls (Ness, 2004).[28] Indeed, aggressive behavior by girls tends to be constructed as an impulsive act, stripping it of its sociocultural context; only violence used by girls in self-defense is consistently explained in rational terms. Clearly, without understanding the value that violence holds for girls in inner cities, our theories about why they turn to violence cannot claim solid ground.

In addition to these subject-specific conceptual problems, the contemporary tendency in the social sciences to partition modern humans separately into psychological, social, and cultural beings has seriously hindered the study of girls' violence. Disciplinary traditions separated by boundaries not easily crossed have long discouraged a simultaneous inquiry into the formal social structure of institutions, the dynamics of culture production, and the psychological development of individuals. This had not always been the case in the social sciences; in fact, the current state of affairs represents a fundamental shift from social science's beginnings in the mid 1700s. While there was much debate surrounding the central concerns that occupied the "new science" at its inception—for example, what it had in common with natural science proper, the methodology for pursuing it, differences in understanding reason and experience, and, most basically, what constituted human nature—there was general agreement about its proper subject: the individual in interaction with a social and material world, as well as with other minds.[29] No divisions were built into its structure to separate individual agents from the social patterns of their environment, as is now the case. Emotional and social life were not partitioned into discrete categories and isolated from history and culture.[30] Rather, the natural and moral worlds were linked together a priori: human and society were taken as a unified field of action and explanation. Epistemologically, human nature itself was considered to be an irreducible category that could not be broken down into constitutive parts without disassembling its essence. The human being could only be conceived of as existing in a social state.[31]

It is only with the professionalization of the social sciences in the late 1800s that sociology, anthropology, and psychology each claimed sole ownership of a particular level of analytical understanding and when the biological, cultural, psychological, and sociostructural spheres began to be considered separately, as if they were each independent entities. From this time forward, even when an attempt was made to bring together ideas that had been staked out by different domains, the cores of these separate disciplines remained distinct. No integrative theory existed with which to build a bridge across disciplines. The result was to omit either the structural determinants that mediate experience or the psychological processes that engender a specific way of making meaning from the vast majority of studies. Thinking about violence in inner cities on one of these disciplinary levels, while a theoretical convenience, does not capture the reality that various levels operate simultaneously to produce a violent event.

With respect to violence, social science has championed either the collective forces that produce violence or the individual risk factors that underwrite individual behavior, without adequately addressing how developmental and sociocultural considerations come together. Until the early 1960s, the idea that social factors played a more instrumental role than individual factors in causing delinquency was considered conventional wisdom (Thrasher, 1927; Shaw, 1930; Whyte, 1943; Cloward and Ohlin, 1960). As crime rates began to climb in the mid 1960s, however, the pendulum began to swing in the opposite direction, and biological and psychological explanations came into ascendancy (J. Wilson, 1975; Wilson and Herrnstein, 1985). But just as it was insufficient to reduce violent behavior to completely economic terms earlier, it was no less unconvincing to reduce its complexity to purely psychological ones later. While over the years some theories of violence of a more hybrid nature have evolved—for instance, racial oppression and displaced aggression theories (Dollard, 1939; Hawkins, 1983) and subculture of violence theories (Wolfgang and Ferracuti, 1967)—even these theories which accept the premise that social and cultural forces act in concert with individual agency do not adequately explain the variable responses by individuals to the same structural arrangements.

To avoid the pitfall of underscoring one analytic level or another, the design of this study had built into it sufficient degrees of freedom to account for both the variation with which girls internalize their surroundings (i.e., taking into account a specific girl's psychological development, her family history, and, where applicable, the girl's history of emotional and physical trauma), as well as the larger sociocultural messages and values that are reinforced within the bounds of her neighborhood. The underlying thesis of this book is that the juncture where the psychological geography of the individual psyche and the social world come together offers the greatest possibility for the deepest insights in studying the incidence of female urban violence.

The Work of Edward Sapir

Although the theoretical and methodological difficulties inherent in considering human experience from a perspective at once sociocultural and psychological[32] has not been a major preoccupation of the social sciences over the 20th century or in the early 21st century, it is important to recognize that neither have such concerns been totally alien from it. There have always been scholars who retained the vision that what was being studied separately constituted aspects of the same reality.[33]

Edward Sapir, an anthropologist who made an important contribution to the personality and culture movement that first began to take shape in the early 1920s, is one such thinker. Sapir attempted to imbue the concept of culture with a processual and dynamic character capable of more accurately capturing the actions of the individual living in a social world.[34] His ideas are especially relevant to the consideration of why girls fight, as they offer a way to wrestle with collective or neighborhood patterns related to violence, while simultaneously opening up a space to consider how individuals in the neighborhood react differently. It is in its ambitious attempt to synthesize these two important analytic levels of inquiry that Sapir's work is particularly useful to my aims in this book.

Briefly stated, Sapir believed that culture and personality were mutually regulatory—that is, that each had a shaping and limiting influence on the other—and therefore it would be a fallacy to study an individual's psychology as if it existed in isolation, just as it would be fallacy to study culture as if the individual had no relevance.[35] Unlike other anthropologists of his day, Sapir did not think that culture, despite its single social frame of reference, was uniformly shared by all members of a community; he rejected the idea that one single version of culture was imprinted onto people as if by a rubber stamp. What was shared, according to Sapir, was a culture's organization, which rested on symbols, and through which people were able to communicate and align themselves toward similar and related purposes.[36] He credited symbols with mediating between the individual and society, as well as with facilitating group cohesion. Thus, people who habitually selected the same symbols and cultural patterns were more apt to experience a sense of psychological identification. These particular ideas of Sapir's are useful in attempting to make sense of why certain girls in the same community fight more regularly than others; both frequent fighters and less-frequent fighters identify with their community, yet their relationship to violence is not exactly the same.

Though Sapir was committed to identifying the ways in which culture was instantiated in personality, at the same time he did not believe that cultural considerations alone could ever explain what happened from day to day; they were inadequate for predicting or interpreting any particular act of an individual. Rather, Sapir believed that individuals in every society represented that society's values differentially and that culture rested on the dynamic process of selective valuation. Said another way, while they were culturally scripted, he viewed individual acts as being organized to adjust to interpersonal situations. Sapir's individual, it could be said, played a part in constructing culture rather than simply being bound by it.

Sapir believed that culture had an important role with respect to regulating the individual, but the individual selectively appropriated culture; it was the vagaries of individual history that drove intrasocietal variation. Thus, while the contribution of culture to behavior was never in doubt in Sapir's mind, it was the individual's interpretation of the collective pattern that he held to be the site of interdisciplinary investigation. In this book, I similarly approach the understanding of how girls within a shared social and cultural context differentially perform violence.

Sapir never lost sight of the fact that the disciplines of anthropology and psychology represented different analytical stances with respect to the same phenomena. He argued that bringing them together would lead to a more accurate rendering of the human condition. Indeed, he believed that it was only through interdisciplinary engagement that a link could be made between the realm of cultural products (shared symbols and values) and the individual appropriation of them.[37] As Sapir cleverly stated, "cooperation between psychiatry and social science best proceeded by starting in the middle and walking in both directions" (Darnell, 1990: 302).

In short, Sapir challenged the idea that behavior was "either" individual "or" social, and he thought it absurd to separate individual from social contributions to behavior since a person mediated both. He believed that all behavior operated from an individual base, at different moments accentuating different functions. How behavior was interpreted—as an aspect of a collective pattern or as an individual reaction—depended on the purposes of the observer. At bottom, however, all human behavior involved the same types of mental functioning—conscious and unconscious—and it was simultaneously social and personal. And as such, he argued, both

the psychological understanding of social behavior and the social influence of psychological behavior could be found in the individual mind.

Here I seek to achieve the same intellectual integration that Sapir sought
well over 50 years ago, specifically with regard to the contemporary issue
of female youth violence in poor urban settings. Indeed, I contend that the
institutional infrastructure of a community (its schools, housing, police
force, and criminal justice system and the configuration of its commercial
economy) the neighborhood culture that is significantly shaped by the limited resources funneled into it by the larger dominant economy, and the
emotional "logic" that resides in the individual living under the confines
and possibilities that the sociocultural environment imposes (a category
that speaks of a collective ethos mitigated by individual qualities)—loosely
mediate the production and reproduction of violent events in a given
neighborhood. These three analytic levels each inform critical aspects of
the relationships among a neighborhood's inhabitants. Although studying
their interaction cannot produce an exact map or formula for predicting
individual behavior, as individual agency is exactly that—individual—it at
the very least attempts to show the interdependence of these three planes
and their mutual influence on one another.

Research Site and Methodology

As the research for this book, I spent almost two years talking to girls
ranging in age from 13 to 17 in a variety of settings: a public high school,
an alternative high school for youth with behavioral problems, the adult
criminal justice system where juveniles are directly filed for any assault
with a deadly weapon, a residential placement center and boot camp, and a
transitional alternative high school where girls leaving placement are sent
before they can return to a school in their community. To gain a window
on the different levels of violence in which girls participate, as well as what
effect the juvenile justice system has on their course, I determined that it
was necessary to observe girls in relation to as much of the institutional
infrastructure meant to deal with their violent behavior as possible. Of the
80 to 100 girls with whom I had contact, I followed 16 closely. I spent time
with two of them several days a week in their West Philadelphia neighborhood to better familiarize myself with their social world. Approximately
75% of the girls with whom I spoke over the course of the year were African
American, 20% were of Hispanic/Latino origin, and 5% were Caucasian.

I also spent numerous evenings doing "ride-alongs" in patrol cars in Northeast Philadelphia in order to observe police and female youths interacting. What this entailed was riding with an officer for approximately four hours at a time. Doing so allowed me to witness for myself the wide range of situations involving girls and their families that garnered police attention—some violent, some nonviolent, but most of the time quite contentious. It also allowed me to see police and female youths interact "in situ," and thereby to better understand the perspective and attitudes of law enforcement personnel as they carried out their duties with respect to girls.

In addition to participant observation and the systematic review and analysis of my field notes to identify themes, patterns, and variations inductively, I relied on relational theory and the Listening Guide Method (Brown and Gilligan, 1992) for conducting narrative analysis.[38] Relational theory has as its central premise that psychological development proceeds through the mechanism of relationships, which are constantly being shaped and reshaped by the social world. The theory suggests that one can best understand internal mental representations and human behavior by examining the interrelationships between persons and between them and their environment. The theory is well suited to connecting the psychodynamic state of a girl who commits violence to the influence of the psychosocial processes that are material to her story. Relational theory has previously, and successfully, been used to study male violence (Gilligan, 1996), with special emphasis placed on the relationship between culture and character.

The Listening Guide Method, a qualitative approach to narrative based on relational psychological theory, systematically attends to the multiple levels of "knowing" within a person by requiring four separate readings of data along specific lines. The act of listening is carefully structured to open a window into the "associative logic" of the psyche—ordinarily the territory of a clinical interview—in the context of the social and cultural world of the speaker.[39]

The first reading serves as a kind of reconnaissance mission aimed at providing an overview of the narrative's plot and a basic map of the speaker's inner world. The second reading, known as "listening for self," observes two basic rules. The first rule is that all statements in an excerpt beginning with "I" are to be considered as a body and taken in the order in which they occur. The reading rests on the premise that the patterns within the narrative are not random but have meaning; thus, their order is preserved to maintain the integrity of the flow of conscious and unconscious material. The second rule is that, by closely observing the use of the first-person "I," sometimes accompanied by only a verb, one can derive insight into how the psychological state of the speaker shifts from utterance to utterance with regard to various themes.

The last two readings are meant to identify specific themes within the narrative—what Brown and Gilligan refer to as "contrapuntal voices"—with the purpose of bringing into focus several of the many psychological states that are simultaneously at play within a speaker at any given time. As identity arises out of messages about the self received from all quarters, as well as from personal introspection, the third reading was specifically employed to identify a host of themes within the social and cultural data relating to how the girls with whom I spent time perceived and experienced their social surroundings. It is geared to identifying important themes associated with the social world that the participants' lives are tied to, with the hope of discerning how psychology, culture, and social structure came together within an individual. For instance, in some cases, the third reading was specifically geared to listening for how an individual pattern of violence fits within a cultural configuration of the neighborhood and then how the emotional logic of a given girl made meaning of this cultural pattern in the context of her personal life history and manifested it in terms of her individual actions. The fourth reading usually takes up a theme of particular importance to a person's individual story.

While the method is not specifically geared to collecting the kind of raw data commonly controlled for in sociological analyses, the interpretation of the narrative as described above indirectly provided information along these lines. The narrative, carefully read, provided such information, as well as an emic interpretation of its meaning. Inasmuch as all interpretations are constructed, the method is also structured to encourage researchers to consider the effects of the interview situation and to take this into account in interpreting the data.

Roadmap of the Book

In chapter 2, I provide a brief description of Philadelphia's troubles as a city, beginning in the 1960s. I broadly trace the deleterious social, economic, and cultural effects wrought by a sharp decline in manufacturing, with a particular emphasis placed on the problem of youth violence. I briefly consider changes to the juvenile justice system in response to the rise in violent crime with which Philadelphia, like most large cities, was hit beginning in the mid 1980s. I discuss in detail the West and Northeast Philadelphia neighborhoods of Melrose Park and Lee where the study was conducted, as well as providing an overview of the study's participants.

Chapters 3 and 4 are in large part devoted to answering the questions, How do girls in Melrose Park and Lee experience causing physical harm, and what meanings do they assign to doing so, including what they see to be the external factors that impinge on them? In chapter 3, I outline the many factors that go into inducing a girl to fight, considering how girls construct and negotiate elements of identity and status through the practice of violence and also what instrumental value that engaging in violence has for them. Additionally, through a range of excerpts, in chapter 3 I illustrate how fighting also solidifies peer relations for girls and provides them with an avenue for the expression of youthful exuberance. Moreover, I consider how street fighting serves as a kind of proving ground for girls to build up a sense of invulnerability and fearlessness (Ness, 2004). In essence, I attempt to provide a sense of what girls' violence "looks like from the street."

In chapter 4, I take up the reasons that girls in Melrose Park and Lee cite for fighting, as well as what actually happens when girls fight. I address the "emotional logic" that underlies and organizes girls' thinking about the resort to violence and show how it dovetails with shared issues surrounding race, poverty, and social inequality. I also consider the instrumental value of alliances into which girls enter with other girls to protect themselves against being physically assaulted or "rolled on" by a group of girls, a topic that is further described in chapter 5.

Chapter 5 is primarily devoted to answering the question, What role do family and peers in Melrose Park and Lee play in socializing a girl to use violence and supporting her image as a fighter? I address the special relationship that exists between mothers and daughters with regard to violence. Nearly every one of the mothers with whom I spoke directly or heard about in my travels had a history of fighting when she was younger, and about one-third of them had yet to stop fighting altogether. The reliance that girls place on peers, female relatives, and even their mothers to come to their aid if outnumbered is an integral part of the anatomy of girls' violence (Ness, 2004). The double-generation dynamic where mother and daughter fight side by side, an important feature of fighting in Melrose Park and Lee, is unique to girls and their mothers with no corresponding parallel to boys and their fathers. In addition to providing a descriptive overview of that phenomenon, in chapter 5 I attempt to explain the function this alliance serves in cultural and social terms.

Why fighting by girls is so commonplace in the neighborhoods that serve as the focus of this book can only be explained by taking into account both larger social realities and local cultural norms—that is, by explaining how structural and cultural forces are involved in shaping individual behavior and how they are involved in shaping feelings (Ness, 2004). In chapter 6, I take up the issue of socialization and child development with regard to performing violence in the context of a neighborhood. I consider how key institutions in the community—school, the criminal justice system, and law enforcement—"construct" and respond to violent girls, as well as look at how issues of race, alienation, and wider systemic forces help structure the social organization of the neighborhood and which, in turn, affect why, how, and when girls resort to violence. Here I contend that many common assumptions about male and female violent youths do not stand up to close scrutiny.

In chapter 7, I offer a concluding statement about how social and cultural factors in these two impoverished Philadelphia neighborhoods produce a proclivity for violent behavior and how these factors are differentially taken up by girls. I make the case that, in disaggregating the levels of culture, society, and psychology analytically, the social sciences have artificially broken apart the study of social problems. Moreover, I underscore that, given the intensive focus that participant observation makes possible, ethnography is particularly suited to accounting for shared social meanings but also to portraying individual inner states. I then offer recommendations for improving policies and practices with regard to female youth violence.

In sum, in this book I explore both the psychological and social worlds of violent girls and develop a structure of explanation that bridges the two. For if there is a dialectical relationship between the social reality of one's world and the "emotional logic" that one resorts to when taking action, then understanding that interaction is essential. Hence, to reach an understanding of what meaning engaging in violence has for a girl, it is equally important to situate the cultural landscape of the neighborhood in which she lives within the institutional framework that has shaped it.

%% 2 *%%*

The City of Philadelphia and Female Youth Violence

Like most major urban centers, Philadelphia is a city of sharp contrasts between wealth and poverty. Most of its struggling neighborhoods, ravaged by socioeconomic neglect and illegal drug markets, lie only minutes from its thriving business district or well-heeled enclaves known for their high-end real estate. Whereas shopping areas in the affluent parts of the city are lined with gourmet-food eateries and specialty shops that cater to middle-class and upper-middle-class tastes and budgets, the main thoroughfares are distinguished by their run-down take-out restaurants and check-cashing places where employees greet customers though bulletproof windows. Beyond what practical implications these differences have for the provision of services to residents, the configuration and use of urban space tells a larger story about the state of public life and economic activity in both types of neighborhoods: the one case suggests vibrant commercial activity and widespread economic investment, while the other suggests severe environmental stresses and the erosion of community institutions. The neighborhoods of Melrose Park and Lee, where the study reported here is set, possess the structural problems and the look and the feel of the latter.

The gulf between the rich and poor in Philadelphia is also immediately obvious to an observer because it is heavily drawn along racial lines. Most inhabitants of Philadelphia's severely impoverished neighborhoods, sometimes referred to as its "inner cities," are African American. Though urban poverty in the United States has never been, nor is it now, limited exclusively to African Americans (even though, indeed, inner cities are currently home to approximately 75% of poor blacks in America), the term "inner city" implies a set of particularly recalcitrant socioeconomic and cultural trends that have had a devastating impact on the residents in such areas, trends that are central to understanding girls' violence.

23

West Philadelphia, where the neighborhood of Melrose Park is located, accounts for nearly 14% of the city's total population, and 72% of its residents are African American. The neighborhood of Lee, in North Philadelphia, is racially and to some extent economically somewhat more heterogeneous.[1]

It is noteworthy that it is only in the early 1980s that the term "inner city" crept into the literature as part of an easily recognizable semantic network used to describe certain neighborhoods in the United States. As cultural studies scholar Charles Acland comments in *Youth, Murder and Spectacle: The Cultural Politics of "Youth in Crisis"* (1995), though never stated as such, the phrase "inner city" was meant to signify, and to be read as, "nonwhite"; over time, the euphemism turned into a formal designation. Needless to say, the socioeconomic and cultural trends that on many levels underwrite the failure of these neighborhoods are central to understanding the unique structure and dynamics of girls' violence. Thus, it is necessary to start by underscoring that the difference in the standard of living between rich and poor and white and black in Philadelphia had not always been as stark as it is today.

From its beginnings, the Philadelphia metropolis, including Camden, New Jersey, was a magnet for manufacturing, given its navigable rivers and its proximity to the shipping ports of the east coast. It was one of the first industrial centers in the United States that could boast a variety of industries. In its halcyon days, after World War II, large employers such as Schmidt's Beer Company, Providence Dye Works, RCA, Baldwin Locomotive, and Campbell Soup Company were focal points of the city's major industries. Of all of its industries, perhaps textiles were the largest (Wikipedia, "History of Philadelphia"). On the Philadelphia side of the Delaware River alone, there were over 700 textile mills that employed upward of 90,000 people at the midpoint of the 20th century (Levins, 2002). Indeed, knitting and a range of small- to medium-size textile mills were once the primary employers in this area. Philadelphia's prime location along central railroad corridors and between the banks of the Delaware and Schuylkill Rivers rendered it a highly opportune place to do business.[2]

Railroad lines running through the city's working-class neighborhoods moved manufactured goods from the conveyor belt to the marketplace, generating steady work for its local population. Entire neighborhoods grew up around sprawling factories, which employed thousands of people.[3] The factories were typically union strongholds where job security and wages were held steady. Row houses, which housed the majority of factory and railroad workers, stretched block after block for as far as the eye could see.[4] Often erected quickly to provide employees with modestly priced shelter close to their jobs, these contiguous, two-story, nearly identical brick houses made it possible for working-class families to buy into the American dream of home ownership.[5] It was not at all uncommon for working-class parents to own their home. Indeed, it is noteworthy that blacks in Philadelphia had a higher rate of home ownership in the second half of the 20th century than in most other cities in the United States, an outgrowth of the economic opportunities that the region's profitable manufacturing sector afforded them.

By and large, the grandmothers of the female youths portrayed in this book speak of "better times" when they were growing up in the neighborhood. While some grandmothers viewed the neighborhoods they grew up in or still lived in as "hard" or "rough," they were unanimous in presenting a picture of a less-dangerous world, one in which violence, while not anomalous, was not a commonplace of daily life. Many of the grandmothers had fought themselves and had firsthand knowledge of what led a girl to fight "in her day." Most saw fighting by girls "back then" as something that was avoidable if the right measures were taken and not as tightly correlated with the feeling of respect and peer acceptance as it is today.[6] Clearly, the symbolic meaning of fighting had changed in important ways, as did the organization of interpersonal violence in their neighborhoods.

For the most part, through to the 1950s and even for another decade or so after that, there was a definable pathway for semiskilled black adults in Philadelphia to move into blue-collar jobs. While workers' lives were built around the harsh imperatives of their job—working long hours operating heavy machinery or working on an assembly line, jobs that were physically demanding and sometimes dangerous—when all was said and done, parents were economically able to support their families. Most workers sent their children to the public school system of the day, which could be counted on to provide the young with a decent education. The idea that children could advance into the middle class was believed to be both within reason and within reach; parents, by example, gave their children the message that almost anything was possible through hard work. Moreover, there was a camaraderie that emerged out of factory culture and with it an extended family network that could be leaned on in hard times. Stated another way, on a number of levels, the abundance of jobs that paid a living wage was the foundation for a safe and stable community. Indeed, about 35% of the nonagricultural work population was unionized in the 1940s and 1950s. These relatively high-paying jobs not only provided income but were a source of respect for the breadwinner and his or her family. While no doubt the effects of respect differ from person to person and family to family, employment in general provided social status and a common set of identifications, values, and commitments that allowed neighbors to generally "communicate" and understand one another.

Philadelphia's troubles as a city began in the mid 1950s as a result of what would later be known as American "deindustrialization"—the large-scale shift from an industrial economy to a service and information economy (McKee, 2004). The city witnessed the loss of more than 250,000 of its manufacturing jobs over the course of three decades (Adams et al., 1991). Essentially, automated and computerized processes came to replace the assembly line and severely diminished the role of piece-workers, too. As in many other American cities, rather than being a temporary setback, the loss of jobs in the manufacturing sector was permanent; company after company closed up shop and left town, sometimes to reopen their doors in a less-populated suburb with a fraction of its original workforce but at other times disappearing altogether. As in other large urban centers, what this amounted to in Philadelphia was the wholesale dislocation of working-class families, in particular, its minority communities. Many a parent of the female youths that I followed could recall one or both of their parents being laid off from their jobs and the difficulties that grew out of the hard times that ensued. Most accounts included firsthand familiarity with a grandparent falling into a downward spiral, bouts of increased violence on the heels of a layoff, or just a sense of general hard times followed by more hard times. There was no shortage of such stories or of painful memories.

To truly understand the scope and degree of urban collapse that Philadelphia was subject to, Philadelphia's narrative of deindustrialization must be considered in the context of its world-class reputation for manufacturing and distribution. It would be fair to say that manufacturing in Philadelphia operated on a grander scale than in most other industrial cities, given its prime geography (on the east coast close to New York City), the advantages of its natural endowment, its enormous industrial infrastructure, and the diversity of its manufacturing base. Historically, the core of Philadelphia's manufacturing base was built around small-scale industries and not large manufacturing plants—for example, while it was the largest producer of textiles in the country, most of Philadelphia's textile products were produced in small shops.⁷ Given the variety of goods that it produced, Philadelphia was commonly referred to as "the Manchester of America," referring to the English town of the same name. Manayunk, a suburb in Northwest Philadelphia, was first bequeathed the label "workshop of the world" in the early 1820s because of the waterpower it supplied to mills and factories in connection with its proximity to canals and dams on the Schuylkill River.

At the same time, Philadelphia was home to large-scale industry. During both World Wars I and II, Philadelphia was a major center of war-related industry. The Philadelphia Naval Shipyard alone employed 40,000 people and figured in the construction of 53 ships and the repair of 574 others at its heyday. After World War I, however, the workforce gradually dropped to around 12,000. By the 1960s, the building of new ships was contracted out to private companies rather than being built on site (Wikipedia, "Philadelphia Naval Shipyard"). When it was officially closed in 1995 as a U.S. naval facility, the Philadelphia Naval Shipyard employed only 7,000 people, almost six times fewer than during the war. A much-higher number of family members were affected by such a severe cutback of jobs.

The drying up of "good" jobs in and around Philadelphia cut the heart out of Philadelphia's local economy. Largely abandoned by business, whole neighborhoods gradually degenerated into zones of severe urban blight. Every time a company closed its doors, the surrounding factory neighborhood was strained just a little bit further. Under the cumulative weight of these closings and the rapidly changing social environment that accompanied them, the city entered into a downward spiral of social and economic collapse. Barricaded storefronts covered with graffiti were a common sight on any block where retail shops once stood. It was not just manufacturing jobs that disappeared. As household incomes decreased and money was in short supply, many long-standing local merchants could no longer generate enough profit to keep their doors open. Residents experienced a severe reduction or loss of local services. Even today, nearly 40 years after the onset and immediate impact of deindustrialization, on any given block in Melrose Park or Lee, it is not unusual to see more shops closed than open. On one street in Melrose Park that I walked down almost every day, there was a take-out restaurant connected to five abandoned stores, which, on the other side, were abutted by a thriving bodega. The bodega clearly offered a range of services, some legal and some not. The boarded-up storefronts in between the take-out restaurant and the bodega included an attorney's office, a "99 cents" store, and a check-cashing place, each of which had very likely known better times. The remaining two storefronts were in such disarray that the identity of earlier tenants could not be deciphered. Left in place of the establishment's sign were graffiti and rust.

Philadelphia's aging industrial stock, which had served it well for nearly 200 years, was a glaring sign of the city's infrastructure breaking down. Unoccupied and left virtually unsecured, abandoned factory buildings were commonly scavenged for scrap metal and any other material that could be sold. Broken windows, exposed foundations, and streets with patches of crumbling asphalt outside the factories were reportedly an all too common sight. A reflection of the social turmoil that engulfed the neighborhood, the old factories were frequently inhabited by indigents or were used as drug dens. For example, the Schmidt's Brewing Factory located in the industry-heavy Kensington area of Philadelphia shut its doors in the 1980s. When the factory closed, 1,400 people lost their jobs (Bleyer, 2000). Once abandoned, the factory became a refuge for homeless people, some of whom reportedly had worked at the company and fell on hard times after losing their jobs. The Kensington Welfare Rights Union, which ran what they dubbed a "reality tour" through the poverty-stricken neighborhood to educate people about the "other" Philadelphia, notes that for years, passers-by could see laundry hanging inside the old Schmidt's factory to dry, especially in the mornings. Several of the girls who appear in this book remembered the old factory on Second Street and Girard Avenue as a place where people went to both do and buy drugs. They recalled how police would frequent the building several times a night when exchanges got especially rowdy. According to many I talked to, gunshots were not an uncommon occurrence. Parents I spoke with had no difficulty recalling the kind of trouble and mayhem that "went down" on Second and Girard, either. Nearly one-half of them personally knew individuals who had either bought or sold drugs at the old factory site. The factory was eventually razed, to the relief of many, as were a large number of the decaying structures that had become a familiar site across parts of the Philadelphia landscape. Many such lots remain vacant to this day, though, similar to a number of other areas throughout the city, signs of redevelopment have appeared in pockets of Lee.

The decline and decay of Philadelphia row houses was also a glaring sign of the city's deepening troubles. In Philadelphia's hardest hit neighborhoods, almost every block was dotted with rubble-filled lots where houses once stood; it took a surprisingly short amount of time for once-thriving neighborhoods to take on a bombed-out look. The massive deterioration of housing stock in Philadelphia's economically battered communities was, at least in part, a function of the contiguous construction of many properties. When a row house collapses or is demolished, its basement often becomes filled with a large amount of dirt and debris. As the walls of the basement are not designed to bear this kind of weight, they tend to bulge out, and eventually they bring down the walls of an adjacent house (Ask MetaFilter, 1999–2008).

Walking through the streets of Melrose Park and Lee, it wasn't uncommon to see two or three houses in a state of total or partial collapse and then one house standing alone that had managed to survive. Nor was it uncommon to see two-family houses with one floor boarded up and the other occupied. According to Tamika, one of the adolescent girls I got to know well and who appears frequently in this book, the boarded-up house attached to hers is a place where "crack-heads got high when the weather was cold." In the warmer weather, the business of the house would also spill onto the sidewalk in front of her door. According to Tamika, frequent calls to the police by her mother produced no meaningful or permanent results to speak of. Recent estimates place the number of houses boarded up by the city of Philadelphia at 40,000 and the estimated number of vacant lots throughout the city at 25,000. Although in some neighborhoods, the number of houses in disrepair dramatically decreased, in Lee and Melrose Park, the numbers are not significantly different from what they were five years ago.

With manufacturing companies significantly scaling back operations or closing their doors altogether, the ability of many working-class families to support themselves in the legal economy simply collapsed. Middle-class and working-class residents who were able to leave Philadelphia flocked to the suburbs in large numbers, with the hope of outrunning the drugs and crime that came with widespread unemployment.[8] Once a primary destination for whites, the suburbs became an answer for many black families who had benefited economically from years of work that paid a livable wage. As a trickle of low-income and welfare housing was introduced to suburban neighborhoods, some poorer blacks were also able to relocate. Although the accommodations open to them in these better-off neighborhoods were far more limited than the ones in reach of their more well-off counterparts, residents of this poorer sector still managed to flee the central areas of urban blight.

Generally speaking, the families that stayed behind were the more economically vulnerable ones and were therefore even less able to manage the heightened economic and social pressures that Philadelphia's working-class communities came under. The "good" jobs that the factories provided disappeared permanently and were replaced over time by service jobs that did not offer the opportunity for class mobility (on this subject, see W. Wilson, 1987). The reduction in income plunged many working-class families below the poverty line and caused extensive family disorganization; as noted earlier, factory work not only made for a good living but was also an important force in the construction of individual and social identity. The story that followed was one heard again and again across many towns and cities throughout the United States. Illegal drug markets began to fill in the vacuum where legal markets once were. Rather than addressing this economic trend as it would inflation or a wide-scale outbreak of an illness, the national government basically relegated the problem to the cities themselves. Rather than investing in new ways to strengthen the infrastructures of such neighborhoods, monies were put into drug enforcement on both the federal and local levels. Some framed the failure of government to come to the aid of neighborhoods that spiraled into decline as malign neglect, while others framed it as the action of impersonal market forces that were wrongly left unfettered. In either characterization, economic instability effectively destabilized the working-class neighborhoods where the majority of Philadelphia's black population had put down roots and lived for decades.[9] The social problems that confronted these neighborhoods were allowed to compound and slowly erode the vitality of local community institutions and businesses and, in time, the neighborhood's vital social safety net.

The term "underclass" was coined in the late 1970s by commentators and entered the popular vernacular in the late 1980s to identify a subgroup of the poor that was ascribed a collective image of danger and moral depravity. Rather than unpacking the complex levels of causation, which seemed to make certain residents incapable of escaping the cycle of poverty—those with a significant character failing that left them unable to compete effectively in a free market—the term served to obscure the structural forces that were inherent to creating such a cycle and provided an easy explanation for the existence of social problems.[10] In this way, the presumed defects in mentality or behavior associated with the individual were made to justify taking harsh measures to ensure public order and security and in the name of civil life. Doing so resulted in the largest expansion of the prison system and the highest rates of incarceration of both juveniles and adults in the history of the nation. Stated another way, individual poverty was not viewed or treated as an outgrowth of structural forces that concentrated poverty in certain neighborhoods. While criminal activity, juvenile delinquency, drug abuse, alcoholism, and suicide were all acts of individual behavior, they were also inextricably linked to a crumbling infrastructure. The focus on individual criminality drew attention away from the need to establish policies aimed at treating the system and conceiving of intervention, not on an individual level but on a collective one. In chapter 6, I talk more specifically about the quality of public schools, poor job prospects for youths, the lack of targeted rehabilitation of youths who enter of the criminal justice system, inadequate health care, and the general undermining of city life and family life as it applies to the girls in this study.

It is within this sociohistorical understanding of how geography, poverty, and demographics have come together since the mid 1980s for the poorest sector of African Americans that an understanding of youth violence in the community must be contextualized. Among the nation's counties, Philadelphia ranked second in population decline in the 2000s—between 1980 and 2000, it lost 10% of its population (U.S. Census Bureau, 2000; see also Downs, 1997). According to the 2000 Census, jobs continued to migrate outward, with only 30% of the region's workers employed within the city limits. The 2000 Census furthermore reported that only 56% of adults in Philadelphia were employed or looking for work in 2000, which made Philadelphia's rate of unemployment the fourth highest among the nation's 100 largest cities. Household income, rates of home ownership, and educational attainment also were reported to have declined significantly since the 1990 Census, as had the size of the middle class. Until the past few years, Philadelphia's statistical report card on itself left little if anything positive to hold onto.

The Problem of Youth Violence Facing the City

Over the course of three decades, the incidence of youth violence increased dramatically against the backdrop of the economic and social changes described above. As businesses closed or left the city for better circumstances, opportunities to find legal employment severely diminished and drug markets made their way into struggling neighborhoods.

It is not surprising that, in response to the economic changes related to deindustrialization, the increase of gang membership and activity proliferated during this period (Hagedorn, 1988; OJJDP, 2001). Indeed, seeing the money to be made, gangs emerged and vied for control of the streets. Signs of gang life became a commonplace in traditional working-class neighborhoods, with drug selling pursued in plain sight. The dangers associated with drug selling became a self-evident fact of communal life in the city. Indeed, the media dubbed Philadelphia the "youth gang capital" of the nation in the 1970s because of the high death toll associated with youth gang violence—on average, during the late 1970s and early 1980s, youth gang violence claimed 42 lives in Philadelphia annually. Gang membership, almost always divided along racial lines, also increased racial tensions in the city—the Crips and the Bloods, which were predominantly black, were the best-organized and the deadliest gangs in the city. Gang fights, which in the past would have been settled with a switchblade, were far more likely to be settled with guns. Gang culture was perceived to be widespread and an insidious force for parents to reckon with.

The greater availability of weapons and, moreover, ones of greater lethality drove the city's homicide rate up and exacerbated the insecurity of neighborhood residents. Juvenile violent crime rates began to rise sharply in the 1980s, much of it drug-related and associated with the appearance of crack cocaine. The result was the creation of widespread fear and dismay among the public about youth and their seemingly more and more gratuitous resort to violence. Again, though the story was not unique for a large American city at the time, it is important to recount here as it set the stage for the future scope, prevalence, and incidence of violence that Philadelphia would be faced with. Efforts to control that violence also must be understood in the historical context from which it arose.

In the late 1970s and early 1980s, female gang involvement was not considered a significant area of research (Campbell, 1993; Chesney-Lind and Hagedorn, 1999). The small body of literature available for that period suggests that the involvement of female youths in Philadelphia gang life was negligible. Female participation, where it existed, was essentially of a supportive capacity: as lookout, weapons carrier, or girlfriend. Indeed, in his study of black female gangs in Philadelphia during the 1970s, W. K. Brown (1977) found that there was only one all-girl's gang that was completely independent of a boys' gang and was engaged in violence. The gang, called the "Holly-Ho's," was said to embrace all levels of violence, including murder. The group was described as taking pleasure in scarring the faces of their female victims and deriving sport from fighting, not unlike girls in Philadelphia who engage in violence today.

Yet, while females in Philadelphia did not exhibit high rates of gang involvement in the late 1970s and early 1980s, arrest records for the period clearly suggest that female youths began to appear in Philadelphia's criminal justice system in far greater numbers. Indeed, for nearly a decade from this time, the growth in arrest rates for female juveniles outpaced male juveniles with respect to most indices that make up the Violent Crime Index and many non-index crimes. This is not altogether surprising, as female youths were exposed to the same economic and social trends associated with deindustrialization that affected male youths.[11] It is noteworthy that in 1980, the violent crime arrest rate for male juveniles was 8.4 times greater than the arrest rate for female juveniles; however, by 1998, it was only 4.5 times greater. Not surprising, given the multiple risk factors that they face, the violent crime arrest rate for female youths was far higher for black female juveniles than for white female youths. In 1980, the arrest rate for black juveniles was 6.1 times the rate for white juveniles; in 1981, the ratio was 6.6 (OJJDP, 2002).

Similar to other large metropolitan areas experiencing a significant spike in youth crime at the time, Philadelphia moved to hold juveniles more accountable for their actions through harsher penal consequences including "mandatory minimums" and, in the most serious cases, by trying juveniles in adult courts. Whereas girls might have been issued warnings in the past, especially if they were first-time offenders, the historical "chauvinistic" leniency of the court seemed to all but disappear for girls in the 1980s. While observers may have disagreed on what was causing the influx of so many more girls into the system, there was consensus that Philadelphia's youth justice system, like others around the country, was not equipped to handle the influx. There were few gender-specific treatment programs or rehabilitative services in either the youth or adult criminal justice system. Funding for programs and services that addressed the unique issues of female youth offenders was all but absent at the time.[12]

Youth violence arrest rates continued to rise in Philadelphia throughout the 1980s until they peaked in 1994, although the application of "zero-tolerance" policies was not repealed even after the rates began to fall. Indeed, with the passage of the 1996 Juvenile Justice Act in Philadelphia, the case of any 15- to 17-year-old minor accused of committing a crime with what was deemed to be a "deadly" weapon was automatically transferred to a special unit for juveniles in the adult court system; the targeted offenses—rape, aggravated assault, robbery, vehicular robbery, manslaughter, or conspiracy to commit any of these crimes—are considered felonies if they are committed by an adult. While most cases directed to the adult unit were eventually returned back to juvenile court, youths were at a minimum fed through a special administrative process. The statute, in combination with judges already meting out harsher penalties to this age group, played a significant role in changing the construction of female violent youths in the court system from delinquents to "offenders." This said, it is important to note that while the trend toward harsher judgment since the 1990s is utterly unmistakable, there clearly has been ambivalence among Philadelphia judges sitting in juvenile and direct-file courts regarding the criminalization of youths. As one family court judge that I spoke with argued:

> It was better when all youths automatically were sent to juvenile courts. That way, the burden was placed on the court to justify sending a youth's case to the adult system, not the other way around. The distinction matters on a number of levels, the greatest of which concerns the message it sends to society about how we think about children.

Another family court judge I spoke with put it even more succinctly: "Legislation gets made based on yesterday's headlines."

The high-profile case of Miriam White, the youngest person ever charged as an adult in the Commonwealth of Pennsylvania, was one that had important ramifications for girls. White, an 11-year-old African American girl from South Philadelphia, stabbed a middle-aged woman to death in 1999, while the woman stood on her front porch. The crime was particularly shocking and heinous because the victim, Rosemary Knight, was a complete stranger to the girl and minding her business at the time. White allegedly took a knife from her kitchen after an argument with a relative and, without a word, went up to the woman and stabbed her. The case was further politically sensitive because the perpetrator was black and the victim was white. The fact that White was female created even greater moral panic in that it reversed conventional expectations about who commits violent and even gratuitous crime—in short, it superimposed the vulnerable image of female as victim on that of female as perpetrator, creating unsettling moral complexity. While the direct-file legislation in Philadelphia pre-dated it, the White case sparked intense pressure for more severe punishment of female youths accused of a violent crime in the city. It served as a reminder of what could happen if lawmakers did not take a firm precautionary stand against violent youth behavior. It essentially became something of a touchstone for proponents of harsher sentencing, with respect to female juveniles. In the eyes of many, White became a symbol of a too-lenient juvenile system where girls were concerned.[13] While White's crime came after the trend toward stricter sentencing laws and practices for juveniles was well under way, both in general and for girls, her crime, with all its attending publicity, put a young minority female face on violent crime in the city.

Although the 1990s saw a significant decline in youth violence in major metropolitan areas, the number of person-on-person crimes in which youth were involved remained relatively high in Philadelphia. This made sense in the overall context of violent crime in the city. The murder rate in Philadelphia peaked in 1990 at 525 and then averaged at around 400 a year throughout the decade (Wikipedia, "Philadelphia"). By 2002, the murder rate fell to a low of 288, but then in 2006 surged again to 406 (Bewley and Hefler, 2006). It is noteworthy that, in 2006, of the ten most populous cities in the United States, Philadelphia had the highest homicide rate, at 28 per 100,000 people (*Chris V's Variety Blog*, 2007). Although the incidence of homicides by females was not a factor in the city's homicide rate spiking, females were increasingly involved in less-violent crimes such as aggravated and simple assault.

The Neighborhoods of Melrose Park and Lee

The Melrose Park and Lee neighborhoods are located on opposite ends of the city, with the downtown area lying between them. Both neighborhoods historically have strong working-class identities—the first within what is known as West Philadelphia,[14] and the second within what is known as North Philadelphia—and have severe problems with poverty, drug use, and crime. In both neighborhoods, nearly 50% of the families live under the poverty line (U.S. Census Bureau, 2000). Indeed, property values in these two locales rival each other for being the lowest in the city.

Older longtime residents who have remained in Melrose Park and Lee typically characterize their neighborhood as being a shell of what it once was and tell similar stories that depict better days. Many remembered their neighborhoods fondly as wonderful places to raise children "back in the day." Perhaps what distinguishes Melrose Park and Lee from each other most clearly now is their racial makeup. Melrose Park is approximately 96% black, whereas Lee is more racially diversified: the breakdown among the major ethnic groups there is 66% Hispanic, 33% white, and 20% black (U.S. Census Bureau, 2000).

Of the two neighborhoods, Melrose Park has a more "bombed-out" look about it and a more consistently lower socioeconomic profile. "Good" and "bad" blocks, identified, among other things, by the number of abandoned houses, virtually crisscross each other in Melrose Park, leaving few if any residential pockets wholly free of the telltale signs of urban blight. On Melrose Park's main commercial corridor, nearly one-third of the stores are boarded up, and many that are in operation keep irregular hours—indeed, one has to travel outside the neighborhood by bus or by car to find a large supermarket, movie theatre, or shopping mall. Within the community, McDonald's, Kentucky Fried Chicken, and Dunkin' Donuts are the only well-known franchise chains to be found. Many of the girls that I got to know frequented McDonald's four or five times a week and celebrated special occasions with their families there. Indeed, nearly every one of the girls that I closely followed had the contents of the different "Happy Meals" committed to memory.

One of the things that stands out about Melrose Park with respect to violence is the opportunities its streets provide for making oneself invisible: ducking into the corner of a vacant lot to smoke a "blunt" (a thick marijuana joint rolled in an emptied cigar casing) or sitting on the stoop of a partially abandoned house to pass around a bottle—the dilapidated state of public spaces in the neighborhood make for easy experimentation with drugs and illicit activities. While police readily make their presence known in the area, that presence is largely associated with surveillance. The police typically respond if a disturbance is called in or drive around in patrol cars with an eye out for trouble, but they make little contact with neighborhood residents otherwise. Despite rhetoric to the contrary, the only consistent presence they provide comes in the framework of an initiative: for example, a neighborhood-wide effort to "take back" certain street corners from drug dealers or gang members. Thus, while to an outsider it could easily look like the police have established a "place" in the community, most people living in the neighborhood perceive the situation otherwise and experience racial tensions as running high.

Within the immediately adjacent blocks from where I spent most of my time, in line with the description noted above, there were few stores in which to leisurely sit down for a meal or a soft drink. The most popular meeting place in the neighborhood for youths was a Chinese take-out store that was open until 4 am every night. In addition to selling food of all types, it sold "loose" cigarettes, rolling paper, condoms, and other necessary accoutrements for hanging out. The establishment acted as a convenience store of sorts, especially in the evenings after most other stores were closed. It quite purposely did not lend itself to socializing, though—it had a bench (more precisely, a ledge) that people would sit on while they waited for their order. If anything, it became a spontaneous crossroad of sorts to meet up with people. Bulletproof glass protected the servers behind the counter with just a thin slot opening for money and food to be exchanged. Thus, in Melrose Park, socializing for youths, if not inside their homes—many of which were run-down, overcrowded with belongings, and not set up for entertaining—was done on the streets. This, without a doubt, had enormous ramifications for fighting, as it commonly meant that a large part of a girl's socializing was done on neighborhood streets without the benefit of any adult supervision. After-school programs for teens, known to be an important tool for reducing juvenile delinquency and crime, while being in high demand in Melrose Park, were unfortunately in extremely short supply.

The idea that violence or crime can occur at any moment is embedded in the running of many institutions in Melrose Park, too. Bullet-proof service windows, like the one in the Chinese take-out, separate consumers from retailers, not only in late-night venues but also in a range of establishments that do their business during the day. Armed security guards are also a common sight in check-cashing places. Bars or gates enclose windows and porches on a large proportion of private homes, even ones that stand in significant disrepair. Thus, even for someone not directly involved in activities that would increase the risk of being exposed to violence, like being in a gang or selling drugs, violence is an unmistakable part of the community ethos, and managing its presence is incorporated into the routines of daily life.

Despite all this, it would be simplistic to say that Melrose Park is characterized by an atmosphere of pervasive threat. Unless a girl is expecting trouble from a situation that is about to occur, she does not walk around feeling or acting overtly scared. Nevertheless, a girl in Melrose Park maintains a certain sense of vigilance to the possibility of something happening. Always being on your guard in Melrose Park is considered to be normative and does not necessarily interfere with youths enjoying the moment when they socialize on the street. Indeed, vigilance, even hypervigilance, has a different meaning in Melrose Park than the one laid out in the American Psychiatric Association's *Diagnostic and Statistical Manual of Mental Disorders*, which defines it as suggestive of an unnecessary level of attention bordering on if not equaling paranoia. In Melrose Park, hypervigilance means being "ready," but not living all the time as if you are in a state of panic or emergency. It means keeping one's wits about oneself and maintaining a reliable compass. In essence, it means "observing."

Even given the range of serious problems that beset their neighborhood, many of the African American families who I got to know in Melrose Park had long and deep ties to the community. As noted, for example, the parents of the girls I followed often grew up in the neighborhood; in many cases, so had one or both of a girl's grandparents. Moreover, although the majority of the Melrose Park girls I followed lived in families with incomes below the poverty level, many of these families owned their homes or, if they did not, had resided in them for several generations. It would be fair to say that, in spite of and alongside the signs of intense poverty that marked the streets of Melrose Park, there is also a coherent, defined, and engaging sense of place and community that speaks of its own vitality and viability. Well-attended block parties are a common sight during the summer and fall months. The smell of barbeque on Sunday is often in the air. These events suggest that connection exists alongside the gated doorways and attitude of "minding one's own business" that characterize the neighborhood, as well.

The neighborhood of Lee, with its high poverty and unemployment rates, weaves a tale of more contrasts. More racially and culturally diverse than Melrose Park, Lee is far harder to generalize about. Historically, Lee was a predominantly white working-class and middle-class neighborhood whose residential sections built up around large companies as they moved into the area. In the 1950s, Lee experienced the "white flight" that most major cities did, along with the government neglect that typically accompanied it—perhaps even worse. Generally, it was Lee's poorer whites who stayed behind, as large numbers of poor and working-class black and Hispanic residents moved into the area. Over time, the neighborhood essentially became redrawn along racial lines, with fairly well demarcated white, black, and Hispanic enclaves, which is how it currently stands today.

Unlike Melrose Park, within Lee, one is able to walk for several blocks without seeing dilapidated or abandoned houses. Well-kept row houses with neat front yards are not an uncommon sight, though certainly they are not the only sight. While in no sense does Lee have a thriving commercial center, it can boast two large supermarkets and a relatively wide variety of well-stocked stores. More franchise chains can also be found, although none of them would be considered high end. One need only walk or drive a short way within Lee, however, to come upon boarded-up houses or a vacant factory building that now serves as home to a bustling drug business. Thus, although a neighborhood hit hard by the consequences of deindustrialization, certain sections of Lee, at least at first glance, appear to have escaped the harsher blows of the economic downturn.

Whereas most of the African American girls I followed in my study lived in Melrose Park,[15] all of the white and most of the Hispanic youths I followed lived in Lee. While I did not spend anywhere close to the amount of time on the streets of Lee as I did in Melrose Park, I spent enough time traveling to and from meeting the girls who lived there to gain a firsthand feel of the neighborhood. In addition, I spent three to four days a week hanging out in schools located in Lee where many of the girls I followed (even those living outside of Lee) attended.

Finally, I spent one or two nights each week in the North Philadelphia neighborhood next to Lee doing ride-alongs in patrol cars in order to observe police and female youths interacting. In these ride-alongs, I got to observe the tense exchange between residents of North Philadelphia and police officers who theoretically were there to protect them. While law enforcement in Lee was officially characterized as being community centered, in practice it rarely seemed to be approached in this way. These ride-alongs also gave me the opportunity to witness how violence in the hands of girls was perceived, not only by the police but by neighborhood residents. It was in Lee during these ride-alongs that I frequently got to see large groups of females squaring off with one another. Although Melrose Park and Lee were by no means the only two neighborhoods in Philadelphia to which my exploration of female youth violence took me, these two places were the central base of that exploration.

The Girls of Melrose Park and Lee

Melrose Park has one of the highest percentages of female-headed households in the city, as does Lee, which contributes to the stage being set for girls in both these neighborhoods to use physical means to stand up for themselves. Homicide rates in each area are among the highest in the city, and the specter of violence is part and parcel of the flow of every-day life. While many female youths eventually find a way to escape the harsh realities of Melrose Park and Lee, until they do, even those who take precautions to avoid "trouble" must be able to protect themselves, should "trouble" come to them. Although the rates of male arrest for violent offenses in Melrose Park and Lee are much higher than the rates for females, the gender gap in both these communities is narrower than in most others in Philadelphia.

The 16 girls on whom I focus differ from each other in terms of home environment, level of intellectual ability, quality of peer relationships, and involvement with the criminal justice system, yet what they have in common is a history of engaging in some degree of physical violence or street fighting (mostly hand-to-hand fighting in a neighborhood's public spaces, though it can include the use of weapons). Indeed, even the girls I met who had not had contact with the juvenile justice system typically reported having been in physical fights over the past year. As one mother put it when I asked her to introduce me to girls in her neighborhood who did not fight, "I don't know one girl who doesn't fight. At some point everyone fights." Most of the girls I spoke with over the course of the year echoed her view, yet there are important distinctions to be made among these girls with regard to the frequency and extent of the physical violence in which they engaged (Ness, 2004), something that I explore further in chapter 3.

My interest was to follow female youths in the course of their reading and negotiating of "the everyday," including the everyday realities of violence, so I could arrive at an understanding of what it meant for a girl to engage in violence. My initial contact was primarily the product of social networking—girls introduced me to other girls, or I struck up a relationship with girls on my own while engaging in participatory observation. Nine of the sixteen girls I ultimately chose to follow closely (Adia, Aiesha, Allie, Cassie, Lakeesha, Manuela, Tamika, and Victoria) attended two alternative high schools for youths.[16] Of these, those attending Paulson (Allie, Aiesha, Cassie, Kia, Lakeesha, Manuela, and Tamika) had been removed from a school in their home district because of serious behavior problems; some of these girls had been earlier remanded to a residential placement. Before a girl was allowed to return to her local school, she was required by the Board of Education to transition through Paulson. New Directions is an alternative high school for youths presenting behavior problems serious enough for them to be removed from their local school, though not serious enough to land them in placement (Adia, Kia, and Victoria). It's important to note that the offense a girl was ultimately charged with and the subsequent disposition of her case was a product of many factors beyond the actual level of violence of her act—some of the girls in New Directions had a history of engaging in more serious violence than girls at Paulson, although they had not been caught or they were met with more leniency in some part of the system. Though many of the girls at Paulson and at New Directions lived in other parts of the city, both of these schools were located in Lee. As noted above, I spent several mornings and afternoons each week as a participant observer in these schools and in the area that surrounded them. For the most part, these schools opened their doors to me and made me feel welcome. I was rarely left feeling that administrative staff or teachers presented a front that would disguise day-to-day life in their schools.

As noted, a large part of my time was spent on the streets of Melrose Park, where one of the girls from Paulson lived (Lakeesha). It was in Melrose Park that as a participant observer I relearned what it meant to spend hours sitting on a stoop engaging in adolescent banter. Moreover, I was able to observe female youths go about the business of staging and "performing" violence without interference from school authorities or treatment facility personnel. Over the course of several months, in some form or fashion, I got "in" with the circle of "associates" that Lakeesha socialized with (Candace, Kendra, and Zalika), which gave me a kind of passport to move with them throughout their neighborhood or wherever their travels took them. There is no way that I could have developed the intimate knowledge of girls' violence that I did without Lakeesha and her friends essentially taking me under their wing.

As my relationship developed with Lakeesha and Candace, I spent time in their homes getting to know their families and their families' friends— what would start out in some cases as contact with four people most close to a particular girl could easily grow to well over ten as the girls' relatives entered the picture. The communication this allowed me with adults, particularly with mothers, also gave me a window on the special relationship that girls and their mothers have concerning violence. Thus, when a fight went down, I often had a working knowledge of the social relations among the fighters, or if not that, of the general networks that they belonged to in the neighborhood. The more I knew about a girl's social network, the better I could contextualize what meaning fighting had for her, not only in terms of the larger collective meanings that influenced her experience of fighting but also in terms of the individual meaning that she brought to it.

Of the remaining three girls whom I followed closely, three (Melissa, Samantha and Shayleen) were placed at Compton-Taylor, a residential facility three hours outside of Philadelphia; these girls all came from the city (one from Lee, one from Melrose Park, and one from a neighborhood in South Philadelphia). Each of these girls at Compton-Taylor was charged with aggravated assault. While all of the girls sent to Compton-Taylor were placed for a minimum of a year, none would be discharged from the facility before 18 months.

I was introduced to Melissa, the only girl in my study to be charged as an adult, by an attorney in the Direct File Unit of the public defender's office. Girls in Philadelphia who were accused of violent crimes in which a weapon was used were automatically passed on to the adult system and had to receive a waiver from a judge if their case was to be transferred back to family court. Melissa had stabbed a male acquaintance in the chest with a kitchen knife. Though the wound was, surprisingly, only superficial, Melissa's case was at first automatically transferred to adult court but was waived back to juvenile court when she agreed to a plea bargain that would place her at Compton-Taylor for 18 months.

Lastly, I was introduced to Natira, a close friend of Allie's, in the course of hanging out with Allie in her neighborhood (Lee). Natira, like several other youths in my study (she, Candace, Kendra, and Zalika), attended a regular community high school.

It is important to note that as a white, middle-class woman, this study never would have been possible had I not earned some measure of trust over the course of a year with the youths I spent time with (most of the girls were African American or Hispanic, as were most of their friends). The trust that developed between myself and the girls I followed did so over the course of many conversations and meetings in which my thinking and behavior were being observed as much as theirs were. It was the result of an accumulation of occasions in which I went the extra mile, be it advocating for a girl with a teacher or probation officer, taking a girl to lunch when she was in the middle of a crisis, or helping a girl with a car ride to her home or to get her hair done.

Trust, however, is not a static phenomenon that can be easily calculated. I must assume that at least some of the time, what I was told as an outsider may have only been a partial truth or a fabrication. As a rule, the girls who talked to me tended to exaggerate their success as fighters and minimize their sense of vulnerability. Also, one of the first things nearly every girl I met would ask me was, "Are you an undercover cop?" Though revealing my university affiliation seemed to put the question to rest on a certain level, I cannot help but think that as I walked with Lakeesha, Candace, and their friends through the streets of Melrose Park, the same question must have arisen for other people in the neighborhood. I would have to assume that my presence, in ways that I do not even recognize, was factored into the situations that did or did not "go down").

Finally, being able to interact one on one with girls in my role as a participant observer made it possible for me to gain insight into the variation that existed within their shared social and cultural settings. Although it allowed me to see how girls changed their views about different things from day to day and over longer periods of time, again, the level of trust that a girl felt with regard to confiding in me also had to be factored into what she told me. Thus, I could attend to the different selves within a girl and also see how our relationship functioned at different points in time to allow me access to a range of her thinking. As noted earlier, though we can learn much from the collective consideration of girls as a subgroup, and such insights are indispensable, individual life circumstances and the psychology of individual girls is also central to understanding why a particular violent incident comes about. It is ultimately at the level of individual agency that the decision to take an action gets made. It is the larger sociocultural factors and cultural norms mentioned above, operating in concert with these personal factors, that lower the bar and make responding with violence acceptable for girls in Melrose Park and Lee.

3

Girls' Violent Behavior as Viewed from the Streets

Why you gonna take me seriously if I don't show you that I'm in charge of myself? That I'm no joke. You ain't gonna respect me until you know that what I say is for real.
> —Samantha, a 14-year-old girl

There ain't nothing more convincing than a good punch.
> —Lakeesha, a 16-year-old girl

This girl tried to really mess me up once. She brought three other girls with her. I knew I was gonna get it, so I cracked her on the side of her face with this can that was on the ground. They thought I was so crazy they just picked up their friend and left me alone.
> —Victoria, a 15-year-old girl

Each decision to fight or not to fight for girls in Melrose Park and Lee has a number of root causes. Some of these causes are systemic: How safe or dangerous is the physical environment? What is the role of "reputation" in preserving a girl's physical safety? How do the constraints of poverty drive the need for an identity as "not a punk"? Does the girl in question have, or envision, a chance to move out of this environment as an adult? What is the involvement of the criminal justice system in the life of a given girl?

Family history also contributes in determining the extent of a girl's fighting.[1] Is the family a stable one? How many adults are present? To what extent is violence condoned, even encouraged, by adults in the family? Does a girl's mother have a history of engaging in violence, and perhaps even her grandmother? If so, does the girl's mother or grandmother continue to fight still?[2]

A developmental component exists, as well.[3] As adolescents, girls are seeking identities as unique persons. For example, younger adolescents, especially, enjoy the "rush" that accompanies fighting, giving their violence an aura of sport. Often, fighting makes them feel powerful and independent in a way that they have not experienced before. With the passage of time, many older girls significantly limit their violent activity, either because that rush has become stale, they have become teenage mothers and view themselves differently as a result, or they look toward a more mainstream adulthood that does not include behaving in such a way.

Finally, individual psychology, the unique character structure and inner world of a girl, plays a large role, too. Some girls experience themselves as victim more than others and need to assert their dominance; other girls are easy-going by nature. These factors come together to play a role in girls engaging in violence in Melrose Park and Lee. Indeed, the convergence is both complex and dynamic, and the elements that obtain are not the same for every girl.

In considering the myriad factors that influence the resort to violence by girls, it is important to begin by underscoring that, while the risks associated with violence in poor urban enclaves are framed usually in terms of males, female youths must daily negotiate their safety on the very same streets (Ness, 2004). As Tamika lays it out, being a good fighter has significant value to a girl living in Melrose Park and Lee:

> If I seem like I'm scared to fight, some girl is gonna think she can mess with me all the time. I mean, even if I don't seem scared, she's gonna try me at some point till she knows how I am. She just better not go crying to anyone that I beat her the fuck up. I hate it when girls go complaining when they lose. They be blaming other people 'cause they can't fight. They should just learn to fight. That's a lot better than expecting that someone's gonna fight your battles for you.

One can hear in Tamika's words a considered weighing of the cultural and social realities of her neighborhood with respect to interpersonal violence. Her assessment leads her to conclude that it is safer for her to fight than not to fight.[4] The excerpt is also revealing of the psychological pressure that she feels under to do so. No matter how Tamika looks at it ("if I seem like I'm scared to fight"; "even if I don't seem scared"), she determines that she must show her mettle. The excerpt also implies that she (and, I suggest, girls like herself in Melrose Park and Lee) must suppress any fear of fighting she may have, as seeming scared could lead to even greater difficulties. Should a girl who feels scared abandon the air of boldness that she projects, she might be overwhelmed by the real dangers that exist on the streets of her neighborhood (Ness, 2004). This said, while a degree of denial can be a useful defense in dealing with an immediate threat, the pretense can also bring forth significant negative consequences if relied on too heavily. Girls in Melrose Park and Lee must strike a balance between projecting a tough exterior to mask fear about their safety and embracing violence as a way of life. In short, the balance depends a great deal on the individual factors associated with the larger factors, laid out above. In any case, being a female in Melrose Park and Lee does not exempt one from the need to signal power or engage in physical aggression.

Certainly, many of the fights that girls enter into in Melrose Park and Lee are immediately tied to self-defense and being provoked—someone "calling out" a girl on the street, a surprise attack, or a show of aggression to an associate or a younger sibling. However, as it is with boys, displaying force even in the absence of danger is also a way for a girl to deter future attack as through the process of fighting she builds a reputation. A good reputation can serve as a deterrent against other girls deciding to "try" her when conflicts arise or against girls just wanting to build their own reputations. As Elijah Anderson, especially, has described, mostly in relation to boys, behavior that appears to an outsider as self-destructive may in fact be an adaptive strategy in relation to the "code of the streets"— a set of "prescriptions and proscriptions, or informal rules, or behavior organized around a desperate search for respect that governs public social relations, especially violence—which operates in drug and crime-ridden pockets of the city where the rules of civil law have been severely weakened" (1999: 9). Anderson's view of violence in such neighborhoods is that it is a survival mechanism or cultural adaptation, rather than a form of social deviance and ethnic marginality—the terms in which youth violence, in Melrose Park and Lee, are usually conceived by authorities and a wide range of professionals.

Within the inner city, the cultivation of a reputation for being violent is one's "capital."[5] In the absence of powerful connections or access to a legal system that does one's bidding, a reputation for handling oneself provides a measure of control. This is no less true for girls. Again, as Anderson has carefully described (1990, 1999), the overdetermined preoccupation with reputation and respect in inner cities is a reaction to the frustration and lack of agency that many residents experience in their everyday lives. The structural constraints that reduce opportunities for mobility in inner cities also undermine opportunities for developing a positive self-esteem. Beyond its deterrent value, there is a psychological economy behind the practice of violence: it serves as a way to be a "someone," especially in the eyes of one's peers. Feeling like a "somebody" becomes the major goal one may set one's sights on. Whether a youngster becomes involved in a non-mainstream network in which violence is a measure of cultural capital is indeed related to a host of complex variables that differ from individual to individual.

Kia, a 15-year-old girl who was sent to New Directions (the alternative high school that accepts youths with lesser problems) after numerous suspensions for fighting and for making threats to physically harm other students, is no stranger to the kinds of situations that go down on the street. Recently, her sister Tanya had been beaten up by a group of girls because she (Tanya) was suspected of flirting with a boy who, according to the girls, was already spoken for. Kia has a keen awareness of the "code-switching" that Anderson (1999) talks about: that is, the move between a repertoire of behaviors that provide security, which are strongly associated with the street, and behaving in accordance with what are considered more middle-class values.[6] Indeed, most of the girls in Melrose Park and Lee with whom I came in contact learn how to turn on and turn off their "street" persona, depending on the specifics of the situation in which they find themselves. They see doing so to be a wise way to handle the dangers and fears generated by their neighborhood as they go about their daily business. With great passion in her voice, Kia lays out her thoughts on the subject:

> I don't think I have a problem with fighting, but maybe other people see it that way. I can handle some attitude, I mean someone gonna be telling me what to do, like my boss at a job, and all. I'm gonna just do what I have to do [to keep that job]. But I ain't gonna take no attitude from no punk cause I ain't no punk. I'm gonna be ghetto if I have to be. My mom always tell me to be smart about when to fight and when not to fight. But she definitely says not to walk away from a fight if it gonna make me look like I can't handle myself. That's the worst thing you can do. One time a girl beat me up pretty bad, and at the end of the fight she gave me her hand to get up 'cause she respected that I didn't turn and run when I saw her coming.

It is noteworthy that, although Kia was transferred to New Directions for fighting (eight fights in one academic year), she has also held the same part-time babysitting job for two years and speaks passionately about opening up a day care center in the neighborhood or even in the area of Center City "where the rich people live." Although her fighting has resulted in her being sent to an alternative school, she has never had involvement with the juvenile justice system. Talking to Kia left me with the sense that she would only go so far when it came to fighting and then would pull herself back before she or someone else got severely injured. She seemed to have a clear enough vision for her future, and she knew that she would jeopardize it if she got in trouble with the law. Thus, while she had to stand up for herself in her current circumstances, she also did not want to allow the possibility of a brighter and more secure future to slip out of her reach.

While adults in Melrose Park and Lee readily spoke, both directly and indirectly, about the alienation they felt from mainstream America and about how the effect of being collectively devalued made the significance of respect become exaggerated in their communities (and increased the likelihood of confrontation), the girls I followed did not make this connection themselves. Nevertheless, the phenomenon appeared to have relevance to them, as well. One can perhaps see this issue being played out in the preoccupation that both male and female youths have with the label "punk." Every girl with whom I came into contact understood that the term "punk" represented the ultimate put-down. Being labeled a punk was the equivalent of being labeled a nobody.

As a developmental period, adolescence is particularly concerned with fostering and claiming a valued sense of self and identity that is constantly being shaped and reshaped as a matter of course (Erikson, 1950; Blos, 1982). For this reason alone, the label would be something to avoid and disavow at all costs. Situations that show adolescent girls in Melrose Park and Lee to be preoccupied with being respected are both commonplace and varied. As Cassie, a 14-year-old girl with an extensive history of fighting puts it:

I hate to be made fun of. Girls be doing that to you all the time. So if you want to respect yourself, you can't let it go. What kind of a person would I be if I just let someone talk shit on me? If I punch a girl in her mouth, she ain't gonna think she can be so cute the next time around. I ain't no punk, and now she know that. Not just her. Now everybody knows that.

Indeed, offering a cautionary tale, Adia, a 13-year-old girl who was sent to New Directions after hitting her teacher, describes her regret over avoiding a fight and the shame she felt for having done so:

> I once walked away from a fight with a girl because I was scared that she was going to give me a good beating. She was bigger than me, and I didn't have any backup, if you know what I mean. So the next day she got me after school. But there was a rumor going 'round for a long time that I was scared to fight, and people be making fun of me. That was much, much worse to me than getting my ass kicked.

It is important to note that although an adolescent girl's concern with reputation is in no way limited to inner cities, the manifestation of that concern in physical aggression to a large extent is. Numerous authors have written about the social and relational expression of aggression that middle-class girls engage in and the significant level of psychological harm that they exact (Crick, Ostrov, et al., 2004; Crick, Werner, et al., 1999; Jack, 1999; Simmons, 2002; Underwood, 2003). Unlike in Melrose Park and Lee, however, "reputation" for girls in middle-class neighborhoods tends to be negotiated in terms of "popularity," through nondirect aggression and other means. Though seemingly less serious, the longevity of such an attack against a girl usually far exceeds the targeting associated with physical aggression. Needless to say, this sort of attack comes with its own set of unique set of dynamics and serious challenges to be faced.

What form violence eventually takes is to a large extent determined by its structuring conditions—the norms that surround it are associated with a neighborhood, the drugs that are used are based on income and accessibility, and the perceptions that arise are based on the scenarios available to the participant. Embedded in the details of a girl's personal story are multiple subtexts about social, political, economic, and cultural realities. The story is mediated through its own ritualized language in which certain conditions and circumstances that are understood by local inhabitants can get conveyed. It would be highly unlikely that a middle-class female living in a suburban setting would tell a similar story about the intersection of violence and drugs as an inner-city female youth would. For example, when Melissa, the 17-year-old girl who stabbed a boy in the chest with a knife, talks about that experience, she tells a story not just about her own behavior but about the social and cultural world in which she lives:

It was a really bad night for me. I had a bad fight with my mother before I left the house. She be giving me grief about not turning out like my brother who is in jail for hit-and-run. He was high and killed these two people, but he really isn't a violent guy at all. I already had a 40 [large Colt beer] before my friend offered me some Angel Dust [PCP]. This guy was trying to kiss me, and when he didn't back off, I got really mad. He left the room, but I was so pissed that I ran out of the house [where she was hanging out and the incident had occurred] and stabbed him in his chest. I don't know what came over me. I saw a lot of blood. My mother made me turn myself into the cops because we knew they'd come looking for me. I never mean to hurt that kid like that.

It just kind of happened, and I felt bad about it afterward. I know that what I did was wrong—very wrong. It just happened so fast, and before I knew it, it was done, and I couldn't take it back.

Melissa's story, while not a common one with respect to its outcome in that most violent acts by girls do not approach that degree of harm, does show how things can quickly get out of control in Melrose Park and Lee where drugs are easily available and many female youths carry weapons. The kitchen knife in Melissa's case was within arm's reach, leading her to cause more harm than she likely intended. While she had fought with weapons in the past, they were rocks and sharp objects that she grabbed off the ground in the midst of fighting. According to Melissa, despite reaching for such objects, she had never hurt anyone badly before. While she reported that she sometimes carried a knife, it was apparently more for show, and she reports never having used it. This is true for many other girls who carry knives, as well—many girls have the perception that to carry a knife is a deterrent to being attacked but do not actually use the knife even when they fight, as long as their opponent does not pull one, either. Although Melissa had never been in trouble with the law up to that point, her brother had similar dealings with the criminal justice system. Melissa's 19-year-old brother was serving a long sentence in state prison for a drinking and driving accident in which two people died. Like Melissa, he had never been in trouble with the law before, either. However, the loss of life that occurred as a result of his reckless behavior resulted in incarceration for a period of no less than 10 years.

While in no way intending to minimize the impact that different social and cultural factors have with respect to structuring how girls come to express and interpret their aggression, one must wonder if the aggression apparent in both middle-class and poor urban neighborhoods, despite their different forms, tells a piece of the same story regarding girls' psychological development.[7] Though some girls learn to mask their aggression and others are encouraged to display it, both scenarios attest to the fact that aggression is no less a part of girls' lives than of boys'.

Indeed, for all the reasons stated above, Melrose Park and Lee are an accepting "cultural space" for girls to fight in. However, when trying to explain behavior, as Sapir suggests, we cannot simply locate patterns in the cultural order but must provide an explanation of how people go about individually making those patterns their own (Darnell and Irvine, 1994: 140). Again, it is important to underscore that the inclination of girls to engage in violence in Melrose Park and Lee exists on a continuum. While the majority of girls with whom I spoke viewed fighting as a way to enhance their security rather than jeopardize it, and most admitted to taking great pleasure in beating up another girl without feeling remorseful afterward, within that commonality, a wide range of intensity and frequency of fighting was exhibited.

While a fight may have "gone too far" for one girl, it may not have given another girl pause. Judgments regarding what was an acceptable level of aggression had a strong personal component among girls. This said, it was rare to hear a girl justify killing or causing permanent physical damage to another girl, even girls who would readily be viewed as being "full of attitude." The far limit seemed to be anything beyond scarring a girl or requiring a girl to need stitches. Up to that point, injuries were mostly described by girls as being "notches on their belt." Lakeesha, a cheerful girl who was sent to residential placement after three encounters with the juvenile justice system, the last for cutting a girl's face with a razor, lays it out:

> I usually be feeling pretty good after a fight. I definitely like how it feels to fight, especially if I mess someone up. No, I don't feel bad because the person deserves what she got. If you're gonna fight, you better be ready to mess someone up or get your ass kicked. You can't say you want to fight and then feel bad about f'ing someone up. That's just not the way it works.

Cassie, currently far more willing than Lakeesha to seize any opportunity to fight that comes her way, echoes Lakeesha's sentiments about not regretting her actions that result in harm:

When I punch another girl real hard, it feels good. The best that I ever did was break a girl's nose. She be bleeding and all and had to go to the emergency room. One time I bashed a girl on the side of the face with a rock that I picked up—she had hit me with a rock also. She had to get stitches, and it left a scar. She had it coming to her. It could have been me who got hurt. Sometimes I be the one that gets hurt, and you don't see no one coming round to apologize to me. I have nothing at all that I'm gonna apologize for.

In essence, each girl assumes that her opponent would likely not show any more compassion if the tables were turned and therefore has little regret over besting her opponent. Rather, the sentiment that gets evoked for most girls is closer to the sentiment "there goes me but for the grace of God." It is with this mindset that many girls view what it means to engage in street fighting. It is the expectation that keeps a girl feeling that she cannot afford to be too sympathetic toward another girl when a misunderstanding arises.

Seeking Out the Fight

Though almost every girl in Melrose Park is at some point called on to show that she can defend herself, even after establishing her reputation, only some girls will engage in fighting on a regular basis.[8] Tamika, for example, a visibly angry girl with a long history of family difficulties, goes to far-greater lengths than most of her peers to provoke a physical altercation. At Paulson for only a month and a half when I first met her, she had already had four fights, two of which resulted in her being physically restrained by school personnel. No doubt, Tamika enjoys the rush that comes just before she fights:

I like getting hyped up before a fight. You know, acting crazy. Talking crazy shit. People be saying things afterwards like that girl really went off. They tell you what you looked like. The shit you said. People they start crowding around waiting to see what's gonna happen. I don't care about how big a girl is 'cause I have a hard punch. It's your punch and how much heart you have which counts the most. I have a lot of heart. Anyone who knows me gonna say that about me.

In this excerpt, Tamika talks about the excitement she feels before and after a fight. It seems that the "crazier" or bolder she gets, the more peer support it brings. While she does not admit to feeling scared, we know from what she has revealed in a previous excerpt that a girl is not really free to do so. One has to wonder if the hyperbole serves to mask or dispel any realistic fear she might have about going up against another girl, especially one bigger than herself. The invulnerability she expresses at the end of the excerpt seems exaggerated and suspect, as if on some level she is working to convince herself.

Like many girls in Melrose Park, Tamika has been fighting for years. She reports that she had her first street fight when she was seven years old. Her family had moved to a different neighborhood, and Tamika felt the girls on her new block were "trying to rule her." These girls would demand that she run errands for them and threaten her with physical consequences if she did not do so. According to Tamika, her uncle, "who had been a boxer," taught her how to "defend" herself, and thereafter she practiced with her brother in the backyard. Tamika says she became "lean and fit," that is, poised to fight, over time; however, here, too, the claim seems more the reflection of a preferred image of herself rather than an actual description of the way things were. While Tamika is no doubt a willing and able fighter, she has certainly suffered her share of defeats, according to her own account. Neither has she refrained from the less-admirable hair pulling and scratching that most girls will deny they engage in when they fight with one another. Other girls at Paulson who were present when Tamika spoke to me said as much. They ribbed Tamika for being less truthful about how she conducted herself in a fight than she contended. Generally speaking, girls alternated between supporting each other's exaggerated claims about fighting and a friendly sparring about how things "really" went down.

Indeed, most girls augment their fighting narrative with exaggerated stories of their prowess and propensity to "get crazy." Peers or associates play a central role in supporting a girl's image of herself as a fighter. There is an unspoken agreement to go along with each other's "hype." Tamika's fighting narrative, largely characterized by authority figures who do not see her side of the story and girls who "ask by the way they behave" to be beaten up, underscores her constant sense of having been wronged and provoked. At times, Tamika will acknowledge that she provokes fights "just because." Girls who fight regularly seem particularly invested in having it known that they can handle themselves (Ness, 2004). Most youths who cross paths with the criminal justice system are picked up many more times than their official record indicates, as witnesses often do not show in court. Tamika notes:

> I've had charges pressed against me seven times, but nothing they had on me stuck. They ain't gonna make me worry about no record. I don't care if I have a record. I'm not gonna let anyone make me no punk. The only thing I hate is being sent to placement 'cause then I'm away from my family and all. Otherwise, I don't care if I got a record.

Tamika's excerpt expresses a sentiment that is common among the girls I followed. Whether a girl wins or loses, if she fights back, she has given a sign to others who might think of fighting her that she will go down trying. Most important is for a girl to show that she will not let somebody walk all over her. Tamika clearly indicates that it is more important in her neighborhood to show that she is not a punk than worrying about the consequences of having a juvenile record. Apart from establishing that she is no punk, thumbing her nose at the potential consequences of having a record in mainstream society, she also delegitimizes that mark against her and, by extension, delegitimizes mainstream society's perception of her. Samantha, a girl sent to placement for resisting arrest and causing the girl whom she was fighting to need 24 stitches, echoes Tamika's words on many fronts:

> I've been arrested. I had three charges against me, but only two stuck. Since I been in placement, I heard that the girl who I messed up don't say no bad things about me no more. She also keeping away from my boyfriend because she knows when I come home I know where she lives. I'd do it again [aggravated assault] and don't care if they send me back here. So what if they send me back. It don't bother me.

Victoria's comment reiterates this general theme and underscores the identity-enhancing function that not "bowing" to anyone plays for her and many girls in Melrose Park and Lee:

> I'm just glad that I stood up for myself, even though they sent me here [placement]. The security guard that put his hands on me [stopped her when he thought that she was shoplifting] didn't have no right to touch me, if you know what I mean. I'm gonna stick up for myself if someone touches me, no matter what. I don't care who he is. It don't matter to me if it's a cop. I'd do the same thing.

Despite their apparent comfort with standing up for themselves by using physical aggression, Kia and Victoria do not have as extensive a history of fighting as Tamika.

It is important to note that several of the girls I followed were sent to placement connected to altercations they had with security personnel in stores. It was not uncommon for a girl to be charged with aggravated assault if she resisted when a security guard tried to detain her. The guard, frequently only a few years older than the girl, often raised in the same neighborhood as her, and poorly trained, would be likely to display excessive control in approaching the girl. As a matter of principle, however, stores looked to press the most serious charges possible in line with a zero-tolerance strategy toward minor offenses. Were a girl to have had previous contact with family court, perhaps for a fight with a peer or shoplifting, the additional charge of aggravated assault would frequently lead to her being remanded to a residential facility.

Tamika, however, far more apt to turn to fighting than Kia or Victoria, had accrued a fairly long list of charges against her in addition to the street fighting she did, which fell below the radar screen and was not detected by the police. During the course of my fieldwork, it was not unusual for Tamika to get into a fight at least once a week or to report that some girl, or group of girls, wanted to fight her. While many of these fights never came to fruition, she was quick to fall into "the talk of fighting": who had wronged her and what she planned to do about it. It would be fair to say that fights did find their way to Tamika as much as she found her way to them. Tamika's fighting was driven not so much by her need to save face or maintain her reputation as by her need to let off steam. Classmates of Tamika generally saw her as "always seeming like she is angry" and quick to "use her hands."

It was an aggressive outburst directed at a subway officer that precipitated Tamika's remand to Compton-Taylor's boot camp division for three months: the officer stopped her for questioning, and Tamika struck him when he grabbed her arm. Tamika had to attend Paulson after boot camp before the city would allow her to return to her district school. It is noteworthy that in 2004, nearly 2,700 students were placed in an alternative disciplinary school in Philadelphia, which was an increase of approximately 1,000 since 2003. These figures do not include students enrolled in "twilight" programs (evening classes) at neighborhood high schools who have come out of placement in the juvenile justice system. Those students are not allowed by law to return to their regular schools, with the idea that they need to be prepared to return to the community. These students number in the hundreds.[9]

The origins of Tamika's "attitude," which she freely admits to having and is proud of—"I ain't gonna change for no one, I don't want to change, I used to be worse"— seems at least in part to be associated with the relational disruptions in her life. She says she learned about having an attitude from her mother, who had a bad drinking problem that often kept her on the streets while Tamika was growing up. Though Tamika says her mother is her best friend now, the relationship with her mother seems to harbor deep ambivalence—Tamika is quick to mention that she "raised herself." She makes no bones about not liking the fact that her mother drank and implies that "her ways" had a significant negative impact on her.

Tamika's father left when she was a baby, and she has only had sporadic and disappointing contact with him since then. He reportedly has had ongoing problems with substance abuse throughout Tamika's life and has spent time in jail for selling drugs, as well. Tamika's father is not the only male relative who has affected her negatively. Her uncle sexually abused her when she was five years old. She only told her mother years afterward, thinking that her mother would not believe her. Tamika's comments about these incidents, as well as other traumatic events that occurred throughout her childhood, suggest that she came to feel early on that she had to stay on her guard or else she would be victimized. Thus, being tough became an integral part of Tamika's self-concept. It became a way of organizing her self-esteem, in addition to any instrumental purposes it held for her living in Melrose Park. A youngster with few good friends, she says:

> I don't need to have friends, and I don't have any. My mom is my one true friend. Even when she was drinking, she made sure to come home to feed us. I don't need no one else. I have my sisters. You can't trust girls. They always be turning on you. So I don't trust anyone except those people who know me from the time I was small and who are close to me. My oldest sister, she watches out for me, and I can call on her if girls are going to roll on me. If you don't get close to girls, then you gonna not get into as much trouble.

One can hear in Tamika's narrative how the denial of her needs for closeness, her general distrust, and the social and cultural climate of the neighborhood she lives in all work together to solidify her drive to fight. For Tamika, like many girls in Melrose Park and Lee, fighting in some sense becomes a substitute for needing others. Her reference to a connection with her sisters, however, reveals the wish for people in her life whom she can trust. In my contact with Tamika's family, I did not sense that her relationship with her sisters was particularly supportive, as she claimed. Tamika's two sisters, at least on the surface, seemed to be unaware of what was going on in her daily life. They were five and four years older than Tamika, respectively, and ran in different circles. Their paths did not appear to cross much at all. This said, there was little doubt that Tamika's sisters would come to her aid in the context of a physical altercation if needed. Although the level of emotional support between siblings varied greatly among the families that I spent time with, a girl, in the majority of cases, could take it for granted that her siblings would back her if needed. While research on the relationship between sibling support and fighting by girls is virtually nonexistent, my impression, based on participant observation, was that girls who received higher levels of emotional support from their siblings, on the whole, seemed less preoccupied with fighting.

Tamika is certainly not the only girl who finds psychological satisfaction and empowerment through physical aggression. Whereas in a middle-class neighborhood a girls' sense of relational disappointment might translate into her socially isolating herself or burying herself in schoolwork, I found that in Melrose Park and Lee, girls frequently sought out a sense of physical invulnerability to replace emotional dependence that was not readily possible. Why some girls had more opportunities for emotional dependence and others less reflects a wide spectrum of personal circumstances, in addition to the social problems that confront the community. In this way, their resort to violence appears to be different from that of boys, though I had far less contact with boys and therefore do not have a full sense of the relationship between the violence that boys engage in and emotional dependence.

The Good Fighter Who Is Willing to Take a Step Back

Though not one to hide from a confrontation, Aiesha (15), an African American girl who attends Paulson and lives in South Philadelphia, manages to avoid more fights than she enters into. This is both because she is generally easygoing by nature and because she is known for not being easily trifled with. It is this combination of popularity and reputation that saves some girls from having to fight constantly. Aiesha has done her share of fighting and no longer feels the pressure to "show herself" to other girls. She has come to see fighting as "being corny—been there and done that." To stay out of fights, she tells me that she basically avoids spending time with other girls outside of school and does not hang out on the streets. Instead, she limits herself to socializing with her sisters and cousins, who feel the same way about fighting as she does. This strategy is not an uncommon one, especially for girls with close and long-standing ties to their nuclear and extended families.

Indeed, many girls I spoke with revealed that they keep a distance from other girls in order to avoid fighting. The tendency reflects a generally held belief that most, if not all, girls are quick to involve themselves in "he-said, she-said" exchanges that end in fighting. Moreover, it speaks of a widely held view among girls that girls cannot be trusted "because they always turn on you." There was almost unanimous agreement among the girls I spent time with that boys could be more easily trusted (Ness, 2004). Girls typically characterized boys as being better able than girls to keep their confidences and as being far less apt to "talk behind my back." Whereas girls typically expressed less trust about a boy's loyalty toward his girlfriend, girls, at least verbally, gave high marks to boys as friends.

This said, Aiesha was sent to Paulson because she banged a girl's head into the ground and "split it open." She didn't like the way the girl "mugged" her cousin (made a face at her). When the girl approached them, Aiesha claims she tried to deescalate the situation, but when the girl continued to bait her, she then "gave it to her bad." A big crowd gathered to watch, and after a while an adult broke things up. Aiesha said she did not care about injuring the girl so badly that the girl had to go to the hospital. She explains:

> She came up to me for dumb stuff. If I wouldn't fight, I'd get my ass kicked. Girls have to be able to defend themselves. They have to be ready. I can't be seeming like a punk. I don't like to fight a lot because I get in trouble and it's a hassle. But sometimes, you just can't walk away. It's like it all depends on the situation. I do what I have to do. It's just the way you gotta be sometimes. I try not to pay mind to what anyone says about it [fighting].

Not dissimilar to Tamika's view of being slighted, Aiesha also feels that she must counter an act of disrespect or face a worse challenge later. She recognizes all too well that in her neighborhood backing down is seen as a sign of weakness and fear. Her excerpt also suggests that she senses a certain pressure to fight, despite how she feels emotionally. Like most girls in Melrose Park and Lee, whether they fight on a regular or limited basis, both Tamika and Aiesha maintain an acute awareness of being labeled a "punk."[10]

From a psychological perspective, what sets Aiesha apart from Tamika is that she has close relationships with her sisters and cousins, as well as with her mother. While her father has been out of the home for many years, he still maintains contact with her. Her mother is a practical nurse, and the family often has dinner together on one weekend day. Still, Aiesha is a good example of how avoiding violence altogether is quite difficult in Melrose Park. Aiesha elaborates:

> While I definitely like how it feels to fight, I ain't no young kid or nothing, and I don't just lift my hands every time someone looks at me the wrong way. I know I ain't no punk, and anyone who knows me knows that. Sometimes a girl who has to prove herself tries to go up against me because she knows even if she doesn't win, she is going to show that she has heart. You know, because she wasn't afraid to try me. So sometimes I have to fight, even if I don't want to. That's just the way it is.

Candace echoes Aiesha's view:

> I do whatever I can do not to fight. I really don't like to fight if I can get away with it. But if you back down, it only gets worse, so if I have to, then I just have to. The last time I fought, it probably came out even. A lot a times you fight to just come out even, and that's ok. You know you say you be the one who won and all, but that isn't always how it is. You just show you ain't gonna back down, and that is basically what matters.

Who gets arrested and placed in an alternative school or a residential facility is to a good extent associated with luck or the lack of it. As briefly noted with regard to Tamika, most of the time girls engage in street fighting, the police do not become involved. Many girls who fight regularly have had no juvenile justice involvement, even though some of their fights have resulted in the physical injury of their opponent. When a fight goes down, people often do not call the police. The injured parties go home to tend to their cuts and bruises privately unless medical care is absolutely necessary. Even when a girl has to go to the emergency room, she does not necessarily tell the truth about how she got her injury, or she may offer no information about who is responsible for it. It is when the police are called to break up a fight that charges are sometimes, though not always, filed. Usually it is the size of the crowd that gathers to see a fight that determines whether the police get involved (Ness, 2004). For instance, Lakeesha cut her sister's face with a razor, but the family never reported it. Allie and Natira are involved in street fights or other delinquent acts a few times a month, and most of the time they have not come to the attention of authorities. As Natira puts it:

I ain't scared of the police. They don't be coming around most of the time unless there is a gun involved or things really get out of hand. I be fighting since I been ten years old, and I never been picked up for nothing. I fight as much as I want to, and nobody gonna stop me if I don't want them to. It's all a big game if you ask me.

Allie also explains:

If you don't mouth off when the police come around, they gonna let you go unless you really fuck someone up bad. Some police lady broke up a fight that I was in near school last week, and she just said that I better go home and stay out of trouble. But then she let me go. I wanted to fight more, but I waited until later and then found the girl again. So I beat her up later and didn't get in any trouble or anything like that with the police. You just got to be smart about it.

Whereas the danger for girls in the street has historically been more closely tied to being sexually victimized, this has changed since the mid 1980s as the overall ecology of high-crime neighborhoods has undergone dramatic change. The burgeoning market for drugs, particularly crack and cocaine during the 1980s, made inner cities more dangerous for females, both as bystanders and as participants. The crack epidemic gave females access to an expanded set of roles in an underground economy, though most of the roles were low level.[11] While female youths in the past may have had more options to distance themselves from street fighting, the pressure to perform violence as a way to increase security has become much greater. This said, none of the girls I followed closely dealt drugs or participated in organized illegal activities.

Interestingly, none of the girls I spoke with cited the fear of male sexual violation as a reason for learning how to protect themselves against physical attack. It is not to say that girls were not sexually victimized by males but, rather, that their need to be able to defend themselves physically was construed mostly in terms of standing up to other girls and as a general approach to standing strong. Although not a common scenario, however, a number of girls talked about the importance of defending themselves in the face of their mother's physical beatings. The girl would reach a critical point where she was no longer willing to be hit by her mother. The girl would either announce this to her mother and threaten, if hit again, that she would hit back or, without warning, surprise her mother with a counterattack. It was not that the girl would learn how to fight in order to fend off the mother. It was more a case of the girl making use of her ability to fight, which was already established, to protect herself against the mother after many years of "taking it." Far more readily, adolescent girls used physical violence against each other.

Fighting as a Matter of Sport and Identity Enhancement

Not every fight between girls in Melrose Park and Lee is related to issues of self-defense. As is the case with boys (Anderson, 1990, 1999), fighting for girls in poor urban neighborhoods provides a venue for identity enhancement. This is not surprising, as identity for most of these girls is negotiated on the street, not in school or jobs, which are scarce. Girls look to fighting to make a statement about who they are and, in some cases, who they would like to become—someone viewed as being able to take care of herself. As Allie, who is perky and quick to smile, explains:

> Fighting is about image. It's about showing you're no punk. I know I don't rule the world, but I can feel like I do, make you think I do. Fighting is independence. I beat someone up if I feel like it.

This scenario is especially the case for young female adolescents, ages 13–15. Fighting in this age range almost has the quality of being instigated as a matter of sport (Ness, 2004). Allie's wish "to rule" has a distinct adolescent quality to it, which reflects the healthy narcissism and the expansive sense of self of youths her age, and it is from this perch that she made her statement. One can also hear how Allie manages her sense of being vulnerable through fighting. Indeed, as a good fighter, Allie has a ready means to feel in power, if only temporarily. Though the wish to feel invincible is also normatively adolescent, it is no less significant that Allie's younger years were characterized by family instability and several traumatic events.

Allie's story is also not unusual for girls living in Melrose Park and Lee. Allie was sent to Paulson after having been remanded to a residential placement facility because she got into a shoving match with a security guard at the mall. Similar to Tamika, Allie "went wild" when the guard "put his hands on her." She had a history of fighting and truancy at school, so the judge sent her to placement for a year. Allie currently lives with her paternal aunt in a well-maintained section of Lee. Her mother left when Allie was quite young because she "couldn't take the stress of raising a kid and was using," according to Allie. Her father, who was a heroin user, mostly raised her. He died of AIDS a couple of years ago but had been debilitated by health-related problems of one sort or another for some time. Allie says that, despite her father's substance abuse and mental health issues, she never questioned his love for her. She explains that she felt she could tell him anything, and he would never judge her. However, it is clear that her father, a Vietnam veteran who suffered from post-traumatic stress, was not always able to provide her with a stable environment.

As I have noted, however, fighting for girls in Melrose Park and Lee cannot be explained solely in terms of their family troubles or individual psychological ills. As with boys, fighting for girls is also a means of solidifying peer relations and expressing youthful exuberance. Moreover, it serves as a kind of "proving ground" to reinforce a girl's sense of invulnerability and fearlessness. As Manuela, a Hispanic girl living in Lee, explains:

It's fun to see fights. It's like watching television. Seeing blood makes a really good fight. Sometimes I like watching girls fight. They pull hair and scratch. They fight like cats. Boys also stand around to see if a girl is gonna get her shirt ripped off or something.

A good example of a girl who uses fighting to generate excitement and bring attention to herself, Allie elaborates on what it actually feels like to fight:

I get nervous before a fight. My hands shake, and my back gets tense. But when I'm done fighting, I'm all hyped. I like the aftereffect. The worst I ever got hurt was when a girl hit me with a pole in the back. It threw my back out of alignment, and I had to go to a chiropractor. I've had black eyes, busted lips, scratches and bruises. Worst I ever gave was three broken ribs. Because I'm white, I have to make sure no one thinks I'm a punk. I mostly fight black girls because they're harder to fight than the Spanish girls.

This excerpt illustrates the progression of psychological states that Allie passes through leading up to and following a fight. In the end, her initial nervousness is transformed into a kind of pleasurable excitement. In it she reveals her mental balance sheet of injuries sustained versus those inflicted, which calculate out to whether or not she is a "punk." Allie is one of two white girls I followed closely; her excerpt also suggests a deeper story about the additional pressure on a white girl to show she can handle herself in her neighborhood. To fit in better, Allie adapts the speech patterns of the African American girls around her and the "attitude" that they project. However, because her father won a lawsuit against the city and was awarded a relatively large sum of money, Allie was able to go to a private Catholic school for most of her elementary school years. With a solid basic education behind her, she seems to have more of a sense than many of her peers that the future holds other possibilities—she readily talked about going to college. Allie seems to turn the swagger and bravado she exudes on or off, depending on the situation. One is left with the sense that she recognizes that the fighting she participates in is not forever. As she notes:

I can't be all thugged-out my whole life, like if I go for a job. But no one is gonna tell me how I have to behave. It's gonna be me that decides how I'm going to act and speak.

The excerpt suggests that Allie is aware of what behavior is considered appropriate and inappropriate by mainstream standards. One gets the sense that when she deems it time to renege her adolescent ways, she will rely on what she learned while in private school and identify with her aunt's professional identity in a "good" job more than with her current identifications. But she makes a point of telling me that she will make this transition only when she decides to do so. It will be her decision and not forced on her by anyone else.

While male youths are commonly viewed in the public eye as resorting to violence more often than girls, on the streets of Melrose Park and Lee, girls show themselves to be far more willing to fight at a moment's notice—an observation strongly corroborated by teachers, the police, and treatment facility personnel with whom I spoke (Ness, 2004). Kia emphatically remarks:

> You kidding me, girls be fighting more than boys do. They so emotional they'll fight over anything. Boys won't get into it over no he-said, she-said. They only gonna fight over something serious like money or drugs. Boys ain't gonna fight because you look at them the wrong way.

Samantha also states:

> I may wait for a little while before I decide to fight someone, but once I get started, I'm gone. Someone got to pull me off the other girl. I keep wanting to go back and get in one more swing. It's like something opens up in me and then that's it, I'm gone. It feels pretty good to get things off my chest like that.

As does Cassie:

> I go crazy when I fight. I just keep on punching and punching. It's fun. Especially when I make the other girl bleed. She ain't gonna forget who did that to her. The last time I fought, it took maybe ten people to get me to stop. I just hate it when someone gives me a look like they think that they're something that they're not. Gonna knock that bitch down to size and she deserves it, too.

As fighting often turns deadly for boys due to the presence of guns, it follows that especially boys who sell drugs will be less inclined to fight over something minor. For girls, frequently, as a girl moves into later adolescence and feels she has "less to prove," her interest in fighting shows signs of waning. Typically, the older girl with a stronger sense of confidence is more willing to walk away from a provocation as long as it stays in the verbal realm. As Aiesha says, "she don't touch me, she can say whatever the hell she wants."

Violence as a Source of Status

It is standing up to a challenge more than anything else that earns a girl a sense of respect among her peers. As long as a girl shows courage, there is no shame in her losing a fight. Whether she wins or loses, she can feel good about herself, as she has shown that she can "take her hits" and has "heart." In this way, as psychologist Sharon Lamb (2001: 215) notes, "fighting back works instrumentally and psychologically for girls in such settings." Far worse than losing a fight is to walk away from one (Ness, 2004). On the other hand, girls who better their opponent are rewarded with praise and adulation. On the subject, Manuela remarks:

> When a fight is about to go down, everyone knows it. Go on the avenue. You run into so and so and fight. Even if you don't want to fight, to be popular you have to, so you just get it over with. This whole big crowd starts to gather, it's crazy.

Manuela was sent to residential placement for 18 months after two assault charges. She used to sell drugs with her boyfriend and especially liked to fight when she got high. She explains:

> Boys like it when girls fight. Girls try to make a fight especially for them. Girls like it, too, because it makes them feel important. Girls are human. Everyone fights in life. Unless you fight, you can't get no respect. I don't have any real difficulty getting respect around my neighborhood and all that. My boyfriend comes to watch me fight when I tell him that I'm meeting someone and there's gonna be a crowd.

Indeed, in Melrose Park and Lee, the ability to "hand out trouble" brings a girl a certain amount of recognition. However, while some research—mostly on gangs—has been undertaken on the instrumental function of violence for adolescent girls, for example, as a source of protection and monetary gain (Campbell, 1984; Brotherton, 1996; Miller, 2001), such work remains the exception and does not amount to a corpus large enough to sufficiently illuminate the issues material to the situation.[12] Again, while the resort to violence by male youths tends to be viewed as instrumental in nature (Bourgois, 1995; Anderson, 1999), female adolescents who engage in violence are rarely depicted as rational actors. Rather, the use of violence by adolescent girls is almost always viewed as being expressive in nature: that is, violence triggered by perceived insults or trivial arguments aimed at decreasing situational tension. This is so even when violent altercations hold similar status significance for adolescent females—for example, fighting over males or to defend one's sexual position (Heidensohn, 1985; Chilton and Datesman, 1987; Chesney-Lind, 1989). As Cassie notes:

> If I think another girl is coming too close to a guy I'm talking to, then she be dissing me 'cause she knows she be crossing a line. The girl be acting like big stuff. So if I don't do something, then she gonna be thinking I'm some punk or something. I'm gonna check her. Once I check her, she don't come back at me so quick the next time. I don't care about the guy because if he wants to go with someone else, that's fine. But the girl just shouldn't be dissing me like that, and I'm gonna let her know it.

In Cassie's excerpt, one can catch a glimpse of how suspicion, a sense of threat and humiliation, and the fear of retaliation conspire to cause a girl to feel she must "put down" another girl. It is not just how Cassie feels about what the girl does. It is also how she will be judged in terms of peer group expectations if she does not "step up." And, indeed, in certain cases, recognizing the use value of a boy's monetary assistance is essential to understanding what a breakup would mean to a girl—a subject that I take up in more detail in chapter 4.

During the year I spent as a participant observer, there was not a single time when a girl admitted to me that she was scared. It was as if there was an unspoken agreement among girls not to acknowledge their fears—"bringing another girl down" typically acted to reinforce a girl's sense of competence. Doing so was also often used defensively to shore up one's sense of desirability.

Several studies claim that aggressive girls manifest social and cognitive developmental deficits that render them less popular (Talbot, 1997; Henington et al., 1998; Ness, 2004). I found, however, that in Melrose Park and Lee a girl's resort to aggression often strengthened her peer ties; girls are looked on favorably for fighting, and fighting enhances their identity status. This is important, as a girl's personal security is based on other girls coming to her aid. A girl who fights is generally seen as a valuable friend to have rather than a pariah, in contradiction to the literature on middle-class girls who engage in physical aggression. As Allie told me about her best friend Natira:

> That girl's my homie; she never gonna let anyone mess me up if she can help it, and I'm the same with her. That's the way that we make sure that each other is ok. That's the way that I know someone gonna be there for me.

As a general rule, it is only when a girl is perceived as not likeable in some way or as fighting for reasons that fall outside of the range supported by other girls that a girl's violent behavior in Melrose Park and Lee is ridiculed by her peers or by her community.

4

The Reasons Girls
Give for Fighting

While on the surface a girl's description of the types of situations that lead her to use violence is straightforward enough ("someone talking bad about my mother," "looking at me the wrong way," etc.), by reading between the lines, one can gain a sense of the emotional logic by which girls justify the use of physical violence. This logic, centered on both an ethic of presumptive retaliation (I do to you first what I sense you're going to do to me) and an ethic of reciprocity (I do for you, and in return you do for me), underlies the formation of social rules that in large part structure girls' fighting. Through contextualizing this emotional logic within the social organization of Melrose Park and Lee, one can get a much better understanding of what girls are communicating when they resort to using violence.

It is not simply that every person in Melrose Park and Lee is only out for himself or herself or that cooperation between relatives and nonrelatives does not exist. However, suspicions run high and are perpetually revived in high-crime, impoverished neighborhoods. Strategies for personal survival in inner cities, where individual and neighborhood resources are limited and everyday life is full of hurdles to be managed, often compete with what Elijah Anderson (1999) has referred to as "civility"—the display of law-abiding behaviors and mainstream values. This, in combination with the perceived lack of interest of the larger society in the decay of its institutions and consequent disorder, leaves many inner-city residents with the sense that they are left to their own devices and must watch out for themselves (Anderson, 1999). It translates to a feeling that the surrounding world must be kept in check and that if one does not strike first, one alternatively will be victimized. The assumption is that trouble of one sort or another can break out at any moment (Anderson, 1990, 1999; Jones, 2004, 2009) and, indeed, is the natural state of things. Generally speaking, trust among individuals in inner cities is something that is hard won, and issues of betrayal and loyalty are constantly in a state of being monitored and assessed. The issue of race relations in America fuels these feelings, and then the real dangers and social problems that plague the neighborhood only reinforce them. The perceptions that develop out of the two have deep ramifications for how people in Melrose Park and Lee live and think about one another.

Troubling neighborhood effects in poor, urban enclaves (i.e., high crime rate, high unemployment, and depression, to name a few) and the sense of alienation that often goes hand and hand with them have mostly been raised in relation to male youths.[1] My research, however, points to the fact that the lives of girls residing in economically impoverished communities are importantly influenced, and their opportunities are no less structured, by the same realities that influence their male counterparts. How girls' lives are affected may, as Sampson and others note (Sampson 2003; Kling et al., 2004), be expressed differently along gender lines.[2] Again, while the girls I followed did not typically make the connection between macro factors and their own behavior, they communicated those connections by their words and by their actions—for example, their presumption of another girl's negative motives, the belief that no one gives you anything worth anything without a struggle, the sense that other girls are going to take what you have if you let them; thus you must take the offensive first to keep that from happening. Many of the girls I spoke with seemed to think that making the first move in a fight was the best strategy, especially if they were not sure of how good of a fighter their opponent was. While a girl can get into more trouble at school for making the first move, in the end, many girls think that it is well worth the consequences in order to preserve their reputation as being aggressive and tough.[3]

Cassie is a good example of a girl who sees things in this way. She strongly adheres to the idea of striking first, as opposed to taking a wait-and-see attitude before displaying her capacity to defend herself. As a matter or style, she is more comfortable letting it be known front and center that she has the capacity to stand her ground and, if need be, ask questions later. Without evident hesitation or self-question regarding her position on the matter, Cassie explains the problem in the following way:

> Girls a lot of the time, they try to mess you up. I'm not really sure why this is. They be jealous or something. This girl started talking bad about me in school. She got a lot of people to think I did some-

thing that I didn't do, so I had to hit her in her mouth so she would stop telling lies about me. I don't need a lot of people being angry at me, and she be starting all kinds of trouble and all for nothing. I could see what was gonna happen if I didn't stop it. It's not your fault if you be defending yourself because someone talking bad stuff about you or someone you care about. It's a way of standing up for yourself when someone starts with you first.

Lakeesha, who says she is willing to walk away from a physical fight more often than not, offers a similar example:

Look, if some girl tries to talk to my boyfriend and all, then what am I supposed to do? I mean, I don't fight to keep a guy tied to me or anything. That's not it. If he wants to walk, let him. But she be disrespecting me when she does that. So he can do what he wants, but I got to show her that I know her game and that she ain't gonna play it on me. Maybe I decide to fight her or maybe I don't, but I ain't gonna let her play me for no fool. No way, no how. Then I deserve what I get. Shit, she just be looking for trouble, and so that's what she's gonna get. She not gonna make me look bad. I ain't no punk. No one bothers me, I ain't going go looking for trouble. I wish girls in my school would just grow up and stop all this stupidness and silliness.

The ethic of reciprocity that girls commonly ascribe to is motivated by the mutual need to have backup if a "situation" presents itself. Girls typically form understandings that they will come to each other's assistance, especially if they are "rolled on" (when several girls ambush one girl or a large group ambushes a smaller group) or if a one-on-one fight turns unfair—mainly, when one party introduces a weapon and the other is unarmed—a tactic that is simultaneously aimed both at "getting" a girl and humiliating her (due to the intensity of the beating she is subjected to).[4]

Just like adults and male youths, female youths in Melrose Park and Lee create personal arrangements to ensure their physical safety, as law enforcement in such neighborhoods is inconsistent at best. Residents usually experience police involvement as creating more problems than they solve. Many of the girls I followed and the adults in their lives had a ready story about implicit or explicit police racial bias, either in the first person or related to someone they knew. The use of offensive language and insults by police officers in the course of their duty is a complaint I heard time and time again. The court system, rather than being perceived by residents of Melrose Park and Lee as a neutral forum, was also viewed to be unfair, leaving people to feel vulnerable. Thus, many residents, young and old, see the best option to be to take matters into their own hands whenever possible and not look to the police or the criminal justice system to provide them with protection or any other kind of assistance.

Along these lines, girls almost always turn to their sisters and cousins to back them, as well as the members of the cliques they "hang" with. While occasionally a boy will be looked to for protection, a girl's security network is almost always exclusively female.[5] In most cases, it would be considered dishonorable for a male youth to physically attack a female peer. Indeed, if a male wants to retaliate against a female, his girlfriend or sister will get involved on his behalf. In fighting another girl for a boy, a girl is expressing loyalty in line with the principle of "watching the back" of people close to her. When she is girlfriend to the boy, the situation may also equate to her stepping in to protect her own interests, as well. Sometimes the girl is simply a friend and sees the situation as an opportunity to be in a fight. The latter example is more the case for younger females ranging in age from 13 to 15, who are more likely to perceive fighting as a way to build their reputation and in the vein of sport.

As a rule, if a girl is known to have good backup, she is less likely to be rolled on. Most of the girls I spoke with either had a personal experience with being rolled on or, if not, knew of a girl who had this happen to her. Each girl I spoke with (and the parents of all of the girls I had contact with) was aware of the risk of being rolled on, and each, in her own way, had come up with a loose plan for dealing with the situation were it to occur. It is important to note that the phenomenon of being rolled on is often surrounded by a great deal of hype, too: while girls have a legitimate concern about being the victim of this kind of an attack, exaggerated and boastful claims about having been the target of a such an encounter are rife among girls. Pride related to having been rolled on is often connected to a girl being able to say that she "got it bad," had the strength of character to pick herself up off the ground, and then summoned her own network of supporters to mete out even harsher treatment than she herself had received. The narrative ends with the girl coming out on top and, in essence, undoing her victim status. Being seen as a victim (that is, a punk rather than simply losing a fight fought with heart against poor odds) leaves the girl vulnerable to further attack, so anything that she can do to reverse that perception protects her reputation and therefore has important instrumental value to her and, indirectly, to the girls she is aligned with.

Kendra, a 15-year-old girl who attends a mainstream high school in Melrose Park and who spends time hanging out with Lakeesha and Candace, expresses a set of views typical to other neighborhood girls her age, with regard to being rolled on. Her basic premise is that having a ready supply of girls to back her up on short notice is tantamount to surviving in her neighborhood. She lays out the logic of retaliation and her own arrangements for striking back:

> There are maybe four girls who I consider to be my "homies." I have them, and they have me—I got them on speed dial. And everyone knows who you got behind you if something comes down. So if you want to fight with me, you better be ready to fight with them, too. I once got rolled on—these girls came and messed me up real bad, but within an hour, I came back with my girls and we got the one girl who started it all and messed her up reaaallly bad. I don't think that she gonna be rolling on me or anyone else anytime real soon. I really don't think she knew who she was dealing with when she decided to come after me. She ain't gonna make that mistake again. I don't fool around. There ain't gonna be no next time, and now she know that.

Lakeesha, who was present while Kendra was speaking, added:

> If you don't have someone you can call on quick, you gonna be in big, big trouble. I got rolled on real bad because the girl thought that she needed a lot of people to handle me because she knows I'm a good fighter. Even if you are [a good fighter], there is only so much you can do if five girls start beating on you. I got plenty of friends to roll with because they want me to roll with them. So we went back that same night and f'd them up real bad. Sometimes, that just be the way it is. Sometimes you win, and sometimes you lose. It's how it is. That's the way that I see it. I mean I rather not be fighting like that and all, but if someone gonna come at me that way, you know, I don't got no other choice.

"Not liking the way a person looks at you" is the most frequently cited reason that younger girls give for why fights begin. On this score, Shayleen, who is currently in placement for aggravated assault, says, "If a girl looks at me the wrong way, I may hit her. I ain't gonna listen to no shit for too long. I don't need to be doing that." It is important to emphasize that, from the standpoint of an outside observer, what constitutes an insult or slight to a girl who is in the mood to fight can almost be imperceptible. Over the course of the many fights that I observed, I would say that it was impossible at least half of the time to figure out whether some affront had been deliberately made or whether there was indeed anything to avenge. However, as I spent more and more time in Melrose Park and Lee, my sense of what it meant for a girl to be perceived as weak became heightened. With that, it became easier for me to identify encounters that had a high potential for being experienced as a provocation, an exposure, or an opening to increase one's standing among other girls. Of course, most girls who grow up in inner cities develop this heightened sense early on. With time, it became clear to me that the combustible ingredient in many altercations between female youths was a real or imagined slight in which one girl was seen as implying that she was "better" than another girl. While self-esteem in this age group is naturally in a state of flux, thus slurs or slights can take on gargantuan importance, a girl's overall degree of security or fragility factors heavily into how a given situation makes her feel.[6]

With great annoyance in her voice, Tamika tried to explain to me the problem she had with a female youth who walked by her in McDonald's a couple of days earlier. It is noteworthy that Tamika neither knew the girl nor had any direct contact with her before that afternoon. In the end, Tamika approached the girl with "attitude," and a fight nearly ensued when the girl countered with her own display of aggressive baiting in return:

> She be swishing her hips and acting all jo [an exaggerated display to bring attention to oneself]. She just gets on my nerves. That's all I got to know. She just be trying to put herself above everyone else, and if I'm in a mood, well, then she gonna pick it up and maybe we're gonna get into something and then gonna fight. Who does she think she is and all that?

Assuring me first and foremost that she was not at all remotely interested in or concerned about what other girls thought of her, Allie squarely sums up the issue in the context of a girl's self-esteem and the importance of her reputation:

If you are pretty, prettier than her, she feels insecure and you can always tell. It's about status. You hate me, you make me.

The ire that a girl unleashes by calling attention to herself based on what she wears, how she carries herself, or the scene she makes in public is related to the perception that she "thinks she's special" (Ness, 2004). The many ways in which a girl can manifest this attitude of specialness seems to be endless. It is not simply the act of pretending to be better than you are that raises the likelihood of a girl being the object of criticism and sometimes much more. Genuinely being prettier, smarter, or in some way standing out seems to heighten the chance of a girl being targeted unless she can simultaneously send the message that her talents do not add up to her thinking that she is above her peers. Thus, a girl can stand out as long as she also presents herself as being "regular" in other ways. One must wonder why a girl in an inner-city neighborhood who attaches a measure of importance to herself inspires such suspicion and animosity.

While no doubt some of the detailed attention paid to slights and the competition that ensues among girls in inner cities is tied up with worries about resource loss, the dynamic that is being described cannot convincingly be reduced to economic and concrete material concerns. As with boys, the cultural significance of respect as it relates to poverty and racism has to be factored into an analysis of the phenomenon for girls.[7] The general emphasis placed on respect has the tendency to make typical age-related preoccupations more intensified. For girls, the issue often gets articulated in terms of self-image and their desirability to boys.

Along these lines, Allie offers an insightful analysis, which speaks to the depth of jealousy and envy that exists among her peers:

It's like, if another girl gets attention, she's taking it away from you. It's as if she's saying she's better than you. So you gonna knock her down a notch. You gonna keep her from making you look bad. You gonna check her, and that gonna make you feel a little better, especially if you be feeling bad about something.

The emotional threat that Allie suggests girls in Melrose Park and Lee experience when they perceive themselves to be upstaged by another girl, while not unique to adolescent girls, points to meanings that are specific to their sociocultural backgrounds and present situations. As previously noted, whereas middle-class girls negotiate jealousy and envy through what has been termed "relational aggression," these same issues in Melrose Park and Lee are staged and settled through force; social aggression here does not act as a substitute for physical aggression (Ness, 2004). While physical aggression is presumed to be a male phenomenon in middle-class communities, relational aggression is viewed more tolerantly, if not as an acceptable channel for girls to express negative thoughts and emotions. It is not the harming of others that is basically off limits for girls in middle-class communities; it is doing so by direct physical means rather than indirect ones.

The literature on relational aggression, which primarily pertains to girls in middle-class neighborhoods, testifies to this (Jack, 1999; Simmons, 2002). In these settings, severe teasing, brutal gossip, and ostracizing are the order of the day, but typically not physical aggression. At least in theory, the aggression that girls inflict in middle-class neighborhoods is discharged in the majority of situations through covert means. As the surrounding community does not positively sanction girls enacting their harmful impulses and intentions, and certainly it does not support their resort to violence, such behavior must remain below the radar screen. Whereas relational aggression can sometimes lead to the enactment of physical harm, when it does, it is more a secondary consequence of the phenomenon rather than being its defining feature—it is the manipulation of relationships to inflict injury that is fundamental to the phenomenon of relational aggression. I am inclined to believe that it is not simply that female teenage jealousies in poor neighborhoods run deeper because of the greater disadvantage that female youths are subject to; rather, the restrictions against girls in middle-class neighborhoods using violence and the consequences to their futures that flow from them are formidable. Middle-class girls are therefore more apt to embrace indirect modes of aggression rather than direct ones.

Another way to understand and frame the ire that girls in inner cities unleash is to consider their attention-seeking behavior as an act of confrontation. Such an interpretation makes a great deal of sense within a context of collective devaluation, where self-esteem is importantly tied to countering the perception of being labeled a punk. In essence, when a girl in Melrose Park or Lee is thought to signal that she is "above" another girl, her behavior is viewed as ignoring the sensitivity to respect that female youths tend to be preoccupied with. This is not a straightforward matter, however, because female friends and acquaintances often encourage one another's boldness and attitude, which then brings attention that can cause a girl to get beat up. The girl who in some way is felt to be aloof or dismissive is most commonly experienced as "asking for it." As Allie suggests, the worry that another girl will outshine you speaks to the low self-esteem that many adolescents in her neighborhood seem to wrestle with.

To be sure, much of the time a girl's sensitivity to being respected plays out around her desirability compared with another's. The dynamic of direct comparison to one's same-sex peers and the competition that surrounds it is not something that preoccupies boys nearly to the same extent that it does for girls. Although boys are also concerned with the issue of "respect," what constitutes "disrespect" for female and male youths is often not one and the same. Indeed, the issues that a female and a male youth's self-esteem are bound to, while they possess some recognizable family resemblance, may be, and often are, expressed in different ways. For example, respect for girls in inner cities frequently plays out in the context of appearance, relational snubs, and, in some form or fashion, relationship to boys. As Zalika, a 14-year-old girl who attends a mainstream high school in Melrose Park goes out of her way to explain when asked:

> Being a girl means you got to be both tough and not too tough at the same time, that is, if you're no lesbian and you want guys to be interested in you. A guy is ok if you fight, but you don't want to be doing that all the time and seeming like some wild thing. A guy won't respect you if he thinks you're out there acting stupid. You want a guy to think that you're a lady but not that you're a sap.

Zalika was quick to add, as most girls do when talking about their interest in boys, that she does not change herself for anyone. Also, that she does not care what another boy or really anyone thinks of her. She fights to maintain her own integrity as someone who cannot easily be intimidated or bowled over. In truth, it seemed to me that there were many more feelings of insecurity than girls wanted to admit to, and fighting was a way to make a girl feel more powerful than she often felt she was deep down. Thus, while status is a significant preoccupation for both female and male youths, "desirability" is one of the major ways in which status is self-measured by girls. Hence, a girl is vulnerable to feeling shame in this area and therefore would be quite sensitive to the reactions of others.

Other reasons that girls cite for fighting are insults to their mother, loyalty to designated others, and venting pent-up rage. Like being looked at the wrong way, the first two are invoked without much provocation. Samantha explains the subject in some detail:

> I'm gonna hit someone if they disrespect my mom—if it weren't for my moms, I wouldn't be here. It's worse than disrespecting me. Your mom is the highest because she raised you. She breaks her neck for you. She gave birth to you. She's the reason that you're here. No matter what, she's still my mom and nothing can change that. Even if I fight with her and curse her out, it don't mean that I'm gonna let someone talk bad about her. You be dissin' yourself if you did that. So it's about a lot of things. You understand? It's a complicated [inaudible] if you don't understand the kind of thing that I'm talking about. It's kind of hard to explain.

Samantha's statement conveys the intense loyalty that she feels toward her mother, despite the fact that her mother has had her fair share of problems, which at times compromised her ability to parent and care for her family. The excerpt aptly characterizes the feeling that many girls in Melrose Park and Lee have toward their mothers. Despite her mother's failures as a parent, Samantha understands that her mother made great sacrifices to raise her, especially after her father left the home. Samantha is therefore willing to go to great lengths to preserve a sense of positive regard toward her mother in the face of all that has gone wrong between them.[8] In my travels I witnessed fewer instances where girls were willing to extend the same kind of unconditional loyalty to their fathers. Samantha on another occasion said as much when I asked her about this directly. After emphasizing how much she loved her father, she said she was less likely to fight someone who put him down. She explained that, while her father had maintained some level of involvement with her over the years, in her eyes he did not deserve the same amount of respect as the woman who bore her and took care of her. She said it was "just different," could not explain why any better, and wanted to leave it at that.

Beyond one's mother and immediate family, loyalty may be pledged to a wide range of associates, though sometimes only on a temporary basis. It is not unusual for girls to move in and out of "understandings" with other girls based on the normal ebb and flow of who is "in" and who is "out" of a clique on a given week. Two girls do not have to be extremely close to back up one another; most girls realize that there is a pragmatic dimension to the arrangement. The arrangement is akin to one hand washing the other: cooperation benefits both. Moreover, a girl knows that if she wins a fight in the service of helping another girl, she is building her own reputation indirectly. Younger girls who pursue fighting as much for sport as for instrumental reasons typically are quite enthusiastic about standing up for others. As noted earlier, many girls are eager to show their mettle and therefore are happy to come by an opportunity to back up another girl, which amounts to another opportunity to fight. Natira, a girl with a ready smile, offers further insight into the pragmatic aspect of loyalty:

> There's this girl on my block that I don't really hang with. But one time she saw me fighting and said that she thought I was a good fighter. The next time I saw her, she said if I would watch her back that she would watch mine, especially since we live on the same block. I have other people at school who I know would be there for me, but if someone comes down on me on my block, I know that I can count on her to cover with me, and sometimes that's enough not to have to fight your way out of something. It's crazy. You don't just look at the girl that you're gonna fight, you look at the girls behind her before you gonna try her. I may feel like I can fight a particular girl and beat her up and all. But if she's friends with certain other girls, I won't fight her. If I can't fight them, I probably won't fight her.

Zalika, a good friend of Lakeesha, who is petite, yet confident about the caliber of her fighting skills, describes a relatively fluid inner circle that appears at the moment to serve her well:

> Last year I had these three girls, and we'd take turns looking out for each other. One moved away, and another I don't really see anymore since she stopped going to the school I go to. So this year I be hanging with another girl from my school, and we said we'd roll together. I been in one fight with her so far, and she's a really good fighter. I mean, really, really good. Like you don't have to worry if she's with you. It's not like I look for a fight or something, but I like knowing who's gonna be there for me if I decide that I'm gonna step up on someone.

And lastly, Victoria, who has been at New Directions for nearly a year, speaks to the sense of fun that often accompanies girls' fighting:

I smacked a girl in the face the other day because she said something nasty about me. I was in the mood to fight, so I just swung. She was totally not expecting it. We both started to fight, and then a counselor came and pulled us apart. I was laughing about it all day with my friends, the way I just hit her and she was so surprised. She was pretty upset afterwards. She's such a stupid bitch. She don't know how to keep her mouth shut. She thinks that she's tougher than she really is, and that's why she got punched in her face.

Girls readily acknowledge that another reason they fight is to deal with pent-up rage. The anger that many walk around with can be related to long-standing family problems or the accumulation of everyday pressures, and it varies from girl to girl.[9] As illustrated above, although a girl will often defend her mother no matter what has transpired between them, she may also harbor intense anger toward her. With few other outlets readily available, fighting becomes a way for a girl to let off some of the steam that builds up inside her. As Allie plainly puts it:

I get mad thinking about my mother doing drugs when I was a kid and not being around, and sometimes it makes me feel like I want to be punching someone. That's not why I fight always, but sometimes I think, especially when I start a fight, it's one of the things that can be going on. It may not be right, but I guess that it is how I handle my feelings sometimes.

Allie's words underscore the progression from thinking about hurts of the past to fighting in the present. The excerpt suggests that fighting can psychologically help Allie feel less victimized. At times, then, Allie uses fighting to undo a sense of helplessness in one area by exerting power over someone she is capable of dominating. In hurting another, it appears that she assuages the hurt that she herself has felt, even if only temporarily and partially. In Allie's case, the source of past hurt is easy enough to pinpoint. As mentioned earlier, Allie's mother left the family home when Allie was very young. Her mother developed an intractable drug problem and never was able to function as a stable parent in Allie's life thereafter. Any contact Allie had with her mother over the years that followed was, for the most part, erratic and disappointing. Indeed, Allie's mother would often make plans to see her and then not show or call to explain why she never came by. While Allie would never say that she stopped loving her mother, on a number of occasions she was willing to confide that she had lost respect for her mother and, at some point, had stopped hoping that her mother would be the mother that she wanted and needed her to be. The admission was not something that Allie would elaborate on when prompted to.

By all accounts, Allie's paternal aunt who raised her provided her with a stable and loving home. Although Allie always felt her father "was behind her," his mental health problems had left him unable to provide her with a stable home. Allie's father died about a year before I met her, when she was just 12. While Allie describes herself as a "happy" person, her difficult family background has left her with many feelings that she has yet to work out. While she was not very comfortable speaking about these feelings directly (not surprising, at her age), I had little doubt that Allie's fighting served as an important coping mechanism for her at times of significant stress and also in relation to disappointment. Although not every girl uses fighting in this way, in Melrose Park and Lee, a large proportion of the girls who fought did.

Kendra, in an uncharacteristically vulnerable state, openly elaborated on her family situation one day when I accidentally ran into her at the Chinese take-out. Her revelation about her mother came after a particularly bad day at school in which she learned that she might be held back at the end of the year:

> Sometimes things feel like they get too much for me, and I just need to let off steam. My mom used to beat me, and she even burned me with cigarette butts a couple of times. She still be my mom though, no matter what. She ain't had no easy life, either, I guess. Sometimes I get to thinking about things, and I know I take it out to the street. I feel like punching someone out right now, but I don't even know why. Nobody better get in my way 'cause they gonna be sorry. Not when I'm in that mood. I'm not gonna listen to anything then. Nothing.

Here, too, the procession from anger to aggression is quite obvious. Kendra is conscious of the fact that she cannot hurt the actual person who has hurt her, so she at times will strike out where she can. While Kendra recalls what her mother did to her, there does not appear to be an opening to directly address the troubles she had experienced in her mother's hands. Yet, although Kendra harbors great anger toward her mother, she nonetheless perceives herself to owe a great debt to her mother. Whatever insults and injuries have muddied the waters between them over the years, Kendra still sees her role as protecting her mother's name. She views coming to her mother's defense as a higher duty, despite how she personally feels.

While the preceding two examples of pent-up rage are associated with mothers who have in some way harmed their daughters, the main source of anger in a girl's life is not always her mother, and it would be overly simple to generalize the phenomenon of girls' anger along these lines. Clearly, mothers are not the only ones who girls feel anger toward. Fathers are often cited as the cause of a range of negative emotions and recurring negative experiences, as are teachers, the police, and various professionals who have passed through the lives of girls (i.e., social workers, probation officers). It is the importance and often the primacy of the relationship between a girl and her mother that makes it so significant on a number of scores and, for that matter, makes the mother-daughter relationship also one of the greatest sources of strength and attachment in a girl's life.

It is likely that more girls who resort to using violence experience sexual and physical abuse than they self-report—around 40% of the girls I followed (in total) acknowledged some history of abuse. Of the 16 girls I followed closely, two reported being sexually abused, and five reported being physically abused (roughly 16% and 35% of my study sample, respectively). While the correlation between excessive parental force and aggression in boys has been well documented in relation to adult male violence (Widom, 1989; Oliver, 1994), the effect of maternal physical abuse on the development of aggressive behavior in adult females has stimulated significantly less discussion. What we do know is that nearly 62% of girls who go on to be incarcerated for committing violence have at some point in their life been physically abused (American Correctional Association, 1990; Beck and Mumola, 1999; Lederman and Brown, 2000). Moreover, in most of these cases, the abuse appears to be part of an ongoing pattern rather than a case of a few isolated incidents (Widom, 1989; Chesney-Lind, 1992, 1997).[10]

Though we can only speculate on the effect of parental socialization, or the absence of parental influence on actual behaviors, there is no reason to think that processes of learning for girls differ dramatically from those of boys when it comes to violence; arguably, learning for both is governed by the same principle of reinforcement. Thus, as abused boys are more aggressive than comparison groups, one would expect that when a girl has been the target of violence and the prohibitions against her committing violence diminish, the likelihood that an abused girl would express aggressive impulses would also increase. While abuse is not a necessary condition for girls in Melrose Park and Lee to seek out and engage in violence, it no doubt can provide insight into certain cases.

In the literature on violence, however, physical abuse has historically taken a back seat to sexual abuse in explaining why females commit violence.[11] When physical abuse is written about in regard to females, this is largely done in a nonspecific way, leaving unclear the exact nature of the abuse, the sex of the offending perpetrator, or his or her relationship to the victim. Moreover, there is little understanding of the dynamics surrounding the abuse and little or no contextualization of its meaning of the abuse in the girl's life, creating the impression that all abuse is equal and can be thought about in that way.

What this boils down to is a body of literature that suggests that boys typically become violent because they are beaten, while girls become violent because they have been violated sexually. While I do not want to in any way minimize the harm that sexual abuse can cause, I would argue that the relationship between childhood physical abuse and later adult violence by females in this framing gets deemphasized at great cost. In that physical abuse of a child by a parent of the same sex is simultaneously an act of victimization and gender socialization, it certainly cannot afford to be underestimated or overlooked. Unfortunately, however, this has been the case. Indeed, developmental research has not adequately examined the role that physical abuse plays in predicting aggressive behavior in girls, in general, apart from inquiring into the specific impact when the girl's mother has been the abuser.[12]

Lastly, while loath to admit it, as noted earlier, girls frequently fight over boys. Even in the early stages of talking to a boy, a girl does not take kindly to another girl getting too close to her interest. In a harsh tone, partly serious and partly kidding, Kia weighs in on the subject, although in the context of why other girls fight over boys, not herself:

> Look, I ain't never fought over a boy and I ain't never gonna do it, but I know that some girls be bugging out when they find that another girl be sleeping with their boyfriend. Whew. . . . You don't want to get near that, believe me. I see girls go crazy over that kind of shit. This shit is serious stuff. You don't be fooling around with another girl's boyfriend unless you ready to deal with what comes next. I know it

happens all the time and everybody does it, but it's asking for trouble
and it's too much trouble if you ask me. If a boy don't want to be with
me only, then he can be with someone else.

Somewhat more willing to discuss her own views, although also insist-
ing that neither would she fight over a boy, Zalika had something she
wanted to add on the subject:

I would be mad if another girl was talking to my boyfriend, but you
know that never happened to me. I don't know why, it just never has.
But it happens all the time, and girls that be mad over that kind of
thing fight a lot. The other day at school a fight broke out between
this black girl and this Hispanic girl over just that kind of a thing.
The black girl says, "You be hitting on my boyfriend and I'm gonna
be hitting you, you dumb bitch." Teachers came and broke it up fast,
and it was supposed to continue after school, but I don't know what
happened after that. That's all I know. That girl knows her boyfriend
be cheating on her before, so I don't know why she think beating up
the other girl gonna make a difference.

Manuela, a girl who readily admits that she likes to fight, also makes it
clear that she will not fight over a boy. However, she makes the distinction
that to fight a girl who is talking to your boyfriend is about "checking" a
girl who disrespects you, not fighting over the boy per se:

I don't care about the guy or anything but I'm gonna mess that girl up
cause she deserves it. The bitch just be asking for it. The way I see it, I
ain't fighting over the boy. I'm fighting the girl because she be acting
in a way that says she thinks I'm a punk.

No doubt, how a girl responds to losing her boyfriend is related to her
personal life history and neighborhood scripts, rules, and roles surrounding adolescent male-female relationships and peer group expectations.
Interestingly, despite whether it is in reality the case, boys typically, and
as a matter of pride, also deny that they would fight over a girl except
when the girl in question is their mother, sister, or cousin. Indeed, it
becomes a matter of pride for a boy to fight when another boy impugns
the reputation of a female member of his family, far more so than when
negative things to the same effect are said about his father. A boy would

likely admit to fighting if something insulting was said about his girlfriend because not to do so would reflect poorly on him. But that is a different scenario than the one in which another boy is suspected of making a move on his girlfriend.

Whether or not female youths admit to fighting over boys, there is no less an understanding among them that "messing with someone's man" is off limits. In practice, however, girls (and boys) move in on each other's romantic interests all the time. Whether the violation is real or imagined, the disrespect that a girl often perceives, and then reciprocates, is enough to start two girls down the path to physical confrontation. Suspicions run as high as they do in part because, while promiscuity is not openly condoned, it is expected that most boys, especially those who sell drugs, will be having sex with several girls simultaneously. Having several girls reflects well on a boy's reputation among his peers. Roger, a 17-year-old boy confirms this. He was a minor drug dealer before he was remanded to Compton-Taylor for 18 months for beating up another male youth so badly that the boy had to be hospitalized. Known to family court over a period of several years, the charges against him had gotten more serious with the passing of time. In his characterization of the situation with girls, Roger in just a few words shines a light on a host of other issues related to the persona he must assume to keep up appearances. He is constantly conscious of the image of himself that he must project. In short, Roger speaks to the instrumental value of having "girls on the side":

> You have to hold yourself a certain way to maintain a certain status. It's all about how people be seeing you. They gonna treat you in a certain way if you come across as being, you know, as being the real deal and not just hype. I like the ladies, so you know I gonna mess around if a girl is hot. It don't mean nothing.

In addition to liking the company of girls, what Roger is also communicating is that, especially if you sell drugs, there is a certain image and lifestyle that you have to keep up in order to be viewed as the real thing. Spending time and money on several girls at once makes a male youth appear like he is a player and not a punk; the message is that he can afford to attract and keep the affections of several girls at once. From the boy's standpoint, his desirability importantly increases with the more females that he can attract and, to a lesser extent, that he can take care of monetarily, in some form or fashion.

Not surprisingly, some of the biggest street battles start with two girls fighting over a boy.[13] Competition over boys in low-income areas clearly can have an added economic dimension that raises the stakes beyond typical adolescent worries or "he-said, she-saids"—girls frequently feel a need to protect their place as a boy's main girlfriend because that role often comes with spending money and a long list of other coveted perks; even boys who do not deal drugs are frequently looked to by their girlfriends for "incidentals."[14] This is especially the case if a girl is the "B.M." (baby's mother)—the mother of a baby produced from a union with a boy—(Ness, 2004). Kia, who recently gave birth to a boy that she named Thomas, after his father, brings home the reality of the matter:

> Derrick [her son's father] buys my son diapers and toys. I worry that if he stops coming around, how we gonna make it. He does some deal-ing, so he got money. Girls see that, so they want to hook up with him. Maybe have his baby so they get him to take care of them. I didn't do that. Me and Derrick had a real thing. No bullshit. We know each other for nearly three years. That's a long time. I ain't gonna let no girl get in the way of that if I can help it. It just ain't right for a girl to do that, but it happens a lot. Any girl gonna protect her interests and not just let another girl take away what it took her a long time to get. No matter what a girl tells you, that's what she's really thinking about.

Despite her earlier cited assertion that she would never fight over a boy, Cassie is an example of another girl with a strong interest in pre-serving her relationship with her boyfriend. Cassie has been with Devon for nearly three years. He buys her things, and she is close to his family. The two spend time at each other's homes and celebrate major holidays together. In addition to the fact that she says she loves Devon, to lose him to another girl would also mean the loss of a measure of financial support. Cassie has grown accustomed to Devon's assistance and factors that into how she gets through the week—she says that Devon likes to see her in "cute" outfits, so he helps her whenever she asks. Her insis-tence that she would never fight over a boy seems to be more a combina-tion of protecting her pride and shielding herself from disappointment in Devon, were he to stray. While Devon has always stood by Cassie, he has also given her reasons to question how truly monogamous he is. Many girls will voice a hard line about not fighting over boys, though, in practice, they will defend what they see as their "turf." Pride and oft-stated principles rebuking the idea of fighting over a boy often fade "when push comes to shove."

What Actually Happens When Girls Fight

As has hopefully been made clear by now, street fights among youths in Melrose Park and Lee are not a rare occurrence by any stretch of the imagination. Fights are frequently set up to "go down" right after school and not far from school grounds. If word spreads that a fight will take place, it is not uncommon for as many as 20 to 30 youths, males and females, to come as spectators. More spontaneous eruptions draw passers-by and are typically not broken up, even by adults, until one party is in danger of being badly injured or humiliated to a point that is viewed as being too extreme. Where that line is drawn depends in large part on the parent, peers, or other observers who are present.

It is not fighting but fighting unfairly that gives a girl a bad reputation in Melrose Park and Lee. Scratching, pulling hair, spitting, pinching, or biting in a fight is viewed negatively. Most girls go out of their way to convey that they do not fight "like a girl." Tamika reveals, "I punched her in her face, and then I banged her head against the ground. I only stopped 'cause someone pulled me off her. I would have kept on going." Kendra confides, "I smashed her in the mouth with my fist 'cause she called me a punk." However, of the many fights I witnessed over the course of a year, few went down as "cleanly" as girls suggested. In reality, girls protect themselves in the midst of a fight any way they can (Ness, 2004). More than anything, how a fight progresses depends on how equally matched girls are. Usually a fight ends when onlookers deem that things have gone far enough—one girl is bleeding badly or is otherwise obviously overpowered. Often, whether winning or losing, girls do not want to stop and need to be restrained.

There is unanimous agreement among treatment personnel, teachers, and police that it is harder to break up girls' fights. Girls are typically described as being more "emotional" than boys and more "devious." Sergeant Palazzo, a police officer with whom I spent many nights riding around in his patrol car, elaborates on this:

Girls just won't let it go. You tell them you're going to take them in, and they get in your face and curse you out. You give a boy a chance to walk, and he does. That's a major difference in dealing with males and females.

Most girls will report that they actually like how it feels to hit another girl, though, again, many will acknowledge that they often get nervous before a fight. Melissa, who tends to approach fighting as sport, explains:

I like seeing a girl get all messed up. You know, they start bleeding [*laughing*] and have to wipe their face. They be all upset and everything, and sometimes they even cry. I don't cry if I get messed up. I just take my beating and walk away. Sometimes I'm gonna try to beat up the girl at a later date, but if I know that she's a better fighter than me, I just let it go.

As previously noted, the regret that one might expect an adolescent girl to feel after she hurts another girl proved to be hard to find among the girls that I spent my days and nights with. Indeed, I found it rare for a girl to admit after the fact that she felt sorry if she hurt another girl badly. For instance, Zalika was somewhat annoyed when I asked her how she felt about injuring a girl she fought. The girl was injured so badly that she had to go to the emergency room. Zalika reports that the girl had to have over 20 stitches. Zalika, with noticeable annoyance in her tone, says:

Why you asking me this? I don't care. She came up to me for dumb stuff. I didn't fight to get my ass kicked. She be stupid, and so why should I feel bad or anything like that? That's not my fault she got messed up.

Zalika's words echo the sense that many of her female peers in Melrose Park and Lee have about doing unto others before they do unto you. Here again, the notion of a competitive environment where one person's success is viewed as being at another's expense can be found. Zalika, like other girls I spoke with, believed it was smarter to aggress first rather than wait to be the recipient of the same behavior. When it comes to standing up for themselves, the question for most of the girls whose paths I crossed is not "if" but rather "when."

Unlike boys, girls ordinarily take a negative view of fighting with weapons: for many girls, using a weapon suggests that one cannot defend oneself with one's own two hands. Most girls claim that they only carry a weapon if they think they are about to be rolled on. However, some carry implements that, while not technically a weapon like a knife or a gun, can be used to cause harm (i.e., a box cutter, flat can opener, or corkscrew). Many girls who carry a knife say that they do so for "show" to deter an attack and have never used it.[15] In addition, girls who usually do not carry weapons may at times do so if they think they are in imminent danger.

When weapons are introduced into a fight, more frequently than not they are knives or a sharp implement that cuts. It is common knowledge among youths that when a girl has a knife, she will likely try to cut the face of the girl she is fighting. Lakeesha, who does not mince words, puts it bluntly:

This way she gonna see herself in the mirror every day and remember what I did to her. She never gonna forget. She not gonna be so bold the next time. Take my word for it. It's not like I'm gonna just go out and cut someone. It has a lot to do with what the other girl is about, too.

Allie elaborates further as to why a knife or a sharp object is typically a girl's weapon of choice:

A girl gonna use a knife to cut another girl because she jealous. She see that girl look prettier than her. Especially if the girl be drawing attention to herself wearing tight clothes. Getting looks from other boys. You're gonna take away some of her power if you give her a scar. This way you don't feel so bad about how you look if you know you're not cute. It's just an insecure thing. For girls, how they look is like everything, so you get them where it hurts when you cut them.

Many of these themes have already been raised before in other excerpts. Of particular issue here is the meaning of a girl's wish to literally cut another girl down to size. Indeed, the commonly held perception that males shoot while females cut was consistently reinforced by the many individuals, male and female, with whom I had contact. Girls' mothers unanimously confirmed this to be the case, as did many of the boys with whom I also spoke. In fact, no youngster or parent who I came in contact with denied the basic premise. Unlike other contentions about raw aggression—which at times seemed questionable—I observed the assertion to be credible and not an exaggeration.

To cut a girl's face in a fight is imbued with symbolic importance. It is a way to extend further one's sense of prevailing by leaving a "mark" in a place where a girl is thought to be most vulnerable. While in reality the act of cutting another's girl's face occurs far less than the stories that surround it suggest—most fights between girls do not result in permanent scarring or injury—even to just talk about one's willingness to do such a thing seems to increase a girl's felt sense of power, belonging, and acceptance. If a girl does scar another girl's face, typically, she will recount doing so as one of her fighting achievements. Little scholarship on the dynamics of girls scarring each other's faces has been undertaken, to date.

It is noteworthy that the boys I talked to were not preoccupied with leaving a mark on their opponent. Rather, boys seemed to be more concerned with using violence as a way to enforce a territorial claim—sometimes it centered around money or proprietary rights of one sort or another, and in many cases it was drug related. For boys, the use of guns had more to do with performing power and increasing one's perceived sense of safety, not marring their opponent's appearance.

Ten of the 16 girls I followed closely reported having at least one fight with weapons. However, again, it is important to note that a weapon could mean many things. Of the ten girls, one said she used a bat, six said they used a blunt or sharp object that was picked up during a fight, one said she used a box cutter, and two, a knife. None of the girls reported carrying a weapon all the time. It would be fair to say that, even though the number of street fights that involved a cutting implement represented a relatively small proportion of the total number of fights, there was vigilance among girls about the possibility that weapons would come into play. Often when girls carry knives, just as when boys use guns, the serious injury that occurs is the result of a situation gone bad and not necessarily one of premeditated and deliberate attack.

5

Mothers, Daughters, and the Double-Generation Dynamic

Rather than being positively reinforced for demonstrating passivity, girls in Melrose Park and Lee are socialized from a young age to "hold their own" and stand up to anyone who disrespects them. A girl's mother typically plays a key role in setting this process in motion. Just as it often falls on mothers as head of household to stand up to an outside challenge—girls' fathers rarely live at home—most mothers actively encourage their daughters early on to fight their own battles so that they will become similarly capable. In fact, mothers and girls in equal number talk of the moment when a girl is told that she must stand her ground in the streets or face her mother's wrath. This does not mean that most mothers want their daughters to fight; rather, they feel that their daughters must be able to defend themselves, given the dangers that surround them on a daily basis. While fathers ordinarily do not discourage their daughters from fighting—they expect them to do what they have to do—as a general rule, fathers play a smaller role in shaping and influencing how girls approach fighting. As Aiesha explains:

> It's different in these neighborhoods. Mothers tell their kids to fight. Way you're brought up. My father said anyone hit me, I have permission to hit back but never hit first. And, if I hit them back, to make it worth it. My mother, she don't want me being scared of nothing. She want me to be able to take care of myself if she's not around. She thinks I should be able to take care of myself just like my brothers. She don't want anyone thinking that I'm soft so they can get over on me.

While a socialization process whereby mothers both stimulate and reward a daughter's aggression is atypical by mainstream standards, and more akin to what transpires between fathers and boys across class and ethnic background, it is in no way anomalous in inner-city neighbor-hoods, especially in African American families.[1] Nor is it a new phenom-enon. Although the messages that African American mothers have given to their daughters about violence have certainly changed in meaningful ways from generation to generation, like any social communication that endures over time, as demonstrated in chapter 4, the mothers of the girls I followed were also well schooled in how to "handle" themselves when they were growing up.

The view and approach to fighting that mothers in Melrose Park and Lee take has everything to do with the socioeconomic disadvantage of their neighborhoods and the structure of social relations in the families that grow out of it. As already discussed, men in Melrose Park and Lee frequently "step off" from both their financial and caretaking obligations as fathers (Anderson, 1990, 1999), the reasons no doubt being complex and multifaceted. Even in cases where individual and family history char-acteristics play an important role in determining a man's employability, the scarcity of unskilled jobs that pay a living wage makes supporting a family in Melrose Park and Lee difficult, at best (W. Wilson, 1987; New-man, 1999, 2006, 2007). Contrary to popular conservative arguments that employed men are less likely to marry women who have their children out of wedlock (because a woman would lose her benefits) (Murray, 1984), I observed that those fathers who lived at home tended to have steady work (Testa et al., 1989), and girls with employed but nonresidential fathers were more successful in school.

Yet, mothers and grandmothers in Melrose Park and Lee frequently become the sole wage earners in a girl's household, often working 50 to 60 hours a week at one or more low-paying jobs. Making matters worse, a high percentage of the jobs that the women work are "off the books": casual jobs that do not provide them with health insurance or other ben-efits. Without a partner to help with child-rearing functions on a day-to-day basis, mothers and grandmothers must also be the disciplinarians and the ones who teach their children how to survive. Overburdened and often overwhelmed, it comes as no surprise that mothers in single-parent, low-income households can find it difficult to closely monitor their children's behavior and environment. This is not to say that males are entirely absent from such households. In many cases, a mother's boy-friend, uncles, or other male relatives live in the family residence, and some fathers who live away come around regularly. However, even when men are present in the home, the discipline of a girl is usually left to her mother or grandmother. It is therefore particularly critical to carefully consider the messages that low-income urban mothers communicate to their daughters about physical aggression. Little, if anything, has been written on the subject from a normative perspective, however, and such an inquiry would be beneficial.

Given the time constraints of many mothers and the harsh realities of the street, mother-child relations beginning in infancy typically stress the importance of self-reliance and a tough exterior; the more nurturing quality of parent-child interactions, such as the direct expression of affection, are commonly relegated to the background. This is not to say that mothers in Melrose Park and Lee do not love their children as much as mothers in middle-class neighborhoods or that empathy and warmth are in short supply. In the absence of a framework that contextualizes the often harsh communication patterns between mothers and daughters in poor, inner-city neighborhoods, however, it can often look and be perceived that way.

Rather, mothers in Melrose Park and Lee typically do not believe in what many of them refer to as "coddling" their daughters; the cultural message is that their daughters are competent enough to stand on their own two feet and therefore should be expected to do so. Indeed, socialization messages that stress the importance of strength and independence are often delivered in a no-nonsense tone of voice. This no-nonsense approach is meant to communicate confidence in the girl's ability to "take it" and to assure anyone who might doubt it that the girl is not "soft." Thus, whether in the context of relaxed banter or related to a serious matter, the interaction between mothers and adolescent daughters can turn loud and confrontational.

Few authors have addressed the normative aspect of this "blunt" style of interaction between mothers and daughters or between female peers in inner-city neighborhoods. One exception worth noting is Niobe Way's (1996) discussion of the subject. Way has argued that, for urban teens, rather than representing a sign of trouble, speaking one's mind and showing anger are an important part of keeping one's relationship with family and peers "real." Rejecting the pathological lens through which a girl's behavior is often viewed, Way has characterized the loud and brassy demeanor of female youth in her work as a positive—the ability to be outspoken, to have one's voice be counted, and, in essence, as reflective of "courage" and "strength."[2] The public boisterous display of "image" embraced by many poor African American girls has in particular been viewed poorly in school settings: girls displaying such behavior are often labeled as conduct disordered, and girls view school personnel as not treating them with respect.[3] Way's work is important in that it argues for the communication patterns of these girls to be seen as something more than an acute display of aggression. It challenges the assumption that the style of communication is necessarily linked to delinquency or other forms of antisocial behavior. It suggests another relational possibility than the one that typically would be concluded under such circumstances.

At the same time, it would be a mistake to generalize uncondition-ally about the positive qualities of such communication or to idealize bluntness in its own right. My observation of female youths in Melrose Park and Lee left me unconvinced that directness always and necessar-ily equated to being real or honest. Loud and angry outbursts between mothers and daughters, or between girls and their peers, while holding out the potential for a greater degree of genuine exchange and intimacy, did not always bring it about. Indeed, girls tended to have a hard time talking openly about their feelings, especially when they seemed most vulnerable. So-called straight talk often reflected discord that was not deeply examined, went unresolved, and, in some cases, was present for a long time. What determined whether the blunt display of a girl's opinions was a communication of real or deep expression had more to do with the relationship to a specific party and the individual personality of the girl. I would argue that what is most significant was the cultural permission that girls and mothers in Melrose Park and Lee had to engage in no-nonsense talk, although the effectiveness of that talk was tied to an array of indi-vidual and familial factors.

Taking the discussion a step further, just as the interactions between mothers and daughters and between peers must be understood on a con-tinuum, it is also imperative to understand how mothers view the necessity of fighting on a continuum. Though mothers typically see the best way to protect their daughters as encouraging them to learn how to protect them-selves, mothers hold differing views about how necessary it is for a girl to go on the offensive. Again, what affects the continuum is the individual his-tory of the mother and other familial variables. Among the mothers I inter-viewed, Aiesha's mother, Ruthie, subscribes to a less-common perspective:

> What you tell your kid depends on the child. I tell Aiesha . . . you don't have to be a hard-ass to get respect. You don't have to worry about what people say. But if someone comes at you, you can't just

walk away from that. If you put yourself in a dangerous situation, something bad is going to happen. But if someone hits first, go back at them. You don't argue if they have a group. Spit in their eye. Grab their privates. Kids can stay out of danger. It's all a matter of how they think about things. It's all a matter of how you tell them to think about things. It's all about how a mother sits 'em down and explains the situation. My mother sat me down, and I sat my girls down, and I suspect that they will sit their kids down when they have kids and they're old enough.

It is no surprise to hear that Ruthie is less interested in promoting Aiesha's readiness to fight—she subscribed to a defensive stance, not a proactive one, as contrasted to many of the mothers I spoke with. This could be because Ruthie is a good 15 years older than most of her daughter's friends' mothers. Ruthie had Aiesha, her youngest child, when she was nearly 40 years old. According to Ruthie, during her teenage years in the mid 1960s, the streets of West Philadelphia where she grew up were not as violent for girls. It is not to say that there were no fights between girls or that gang life, which was prominent in her day, did not make the streets of her neighborhood somewhat unsafe or like a maze to be navigated. According to Ruthie, the frequency and degree of violence today is different from what it had been, both generally speaking and specifically, when it comes to girls. The pressure on girls to fight was far less, and the stakes were also far less. Only in rare cases did a girl have to worry that if she rubbed someone the wrong way she could be putting her life in jeopardy.

Ruthie explains that, in her day, if a girl wanted to, she could pretty much avoid fighting. Whether or not a girl fought had much to do with whether the girl was in a gang, if she liked to fight, and, at bottom, the life circumstances of the individual girl. While gang life was a reality and real force of the community, it did not have to be a part of growing up for a female youngster. According to Ruthie, an "attitude" helped a girl communicate to others that she could "handle" herself, and a lot of the time, that was all a girl needed to do to deflect trouble coming her way. These days, however, Ruthie describes the situation differently. She concedes that, whereas a girl can limit her fighting if she is smart and driven toward her future, nowadays, a girl still has to prove her ability to defend herself in some form or fashion; otherwise, she is more vulnerable to being harassed and preyed on by other girls. For Ruthie, this is a major difference between her day and that of her children's. Ruthie was clearly disturbed and sad-dened by the changes in her neighborhood and seemed to have a sense of nostalgia when she spoke about the Melrose Park of her past.

It is important to note that while Aiesha is a good fighter and fights much less than many of the girls I followed, Aiesha's older sister Tisha has a completely different profile when it comes to fighting. As Ruthie put it, from a young age, Tisha was both a rebel and a "warrior." Tisha associated with peers who readily embraced violence and gravitated toward the kind of drug use that impaired or ruined futures. She never finished high school and was arrested for drug possession on two occa-sions, the last time resulting in a short stay in the county jail. Despite the fact that Ruthie gave the same message to both of her daughters about fighting, it is anything but unusual for siblings in the same family to have different trajectories with respect to violence. Indeed, examples of the so-called good child/bad child phenomenon within families in Melrose Park and Lee exist in abundant supply. In my study alone, that was apparent. Unfortunately, social science literature offers minimal insight into differ-ential sibling adjustment and outcomes with respect to psychosocial risks in poor urban settings, and additional research in this area indeed would be relevant and useful.

Whereas Aiesha tries to keep her distance from violence, Tisha far more readily has accepted violence into her life. When asked why she thought her daughters turned out so differently, Ruthie explained Tisha's lifestyle in the context of the disappointments the girl suffered in relation to her biological father. While Aiesha's biological father, who did not live in the home for many years, had always filled a positive role in her life, Tisha's (different) biological father had a substance abuse problem and only visited her erratically. Clearly, delivering the "right" message about violence did not guarantee that a daughter would overcome the other negative forces that entered into her life. Factors beyond parental influ-ence that shape individual behavior—factors in the environment other than differential parenting—must of course be taken into consideration (Manke et al., 1995). In Tisha's case, the mix of individual, familial, and sociocultural factors resulted in a troubled outcome; with Aiesha, there were fewer mine fields to negotiate. With obvious upset and consterna-tion in her voice, Ruthie explains:

> I worry about my Tisha because she is not settled inside herself. She
> is much better since she started working a few months ago over at

the Home Depot. She be trying to turn herself around, and I pray that she can do that before she does herself more harm. There is a lot of stupid people who can cause you trouble around here.

At the other end of the spectrum, Lakeesha's mother, Fazia, talks candidly about the importance of her girls being ready or "prepared." Fazia does not only think that a girl must know how to defend herself if trouble happens to find her. Depending on the situation, she sees the importance of a girl being the aggressor—where to do so would be the far smarter course of action. Exhibiting careful thought about the matter, Fazia explains:

Sometimes kids fight not to be disrespected. You pick on a kid, the kid is gonna feel small. He or she has to fight. Tired of rude comments. Only thing can do is fight. If you keep on letting someone do that to you, they'll keep on doing it. Girls have to be rougher than boys are. Have more to protect. Can't let themselves be stepped on, used, taken advantage of. They have to make it clear who they are and what they gonna do if someone crosses a line on them. They have to anticipate trouble even before it happens. It's kind of always been that way. A girl has to stand her ground, not just boys, and don't let anyone tell you otherwise because it's just not true.

In remarking that girls have more to protect, Fazia here is alluding to the additional risk that a girl faces of being raped. It was my sense, however, that she also was referencing the reality that many mothers talked about: that females must manage their lives without a male helping out—in essence, that, in Melrose Park and Lee, the buck stops with a woman, not a man. Thus, girls must be ready for "all the shit that goes down." Not surprisingly, Fazia's daughter Lakeesha holds this perspective, as well:

Fighting not really gonna solve no problem, but it gonna give someone the message that they can't just walk all over you. Once you make that clear, it gonna be easier for you. That's just the way it is around here, and everybody knows it. And that's that. That's just how it is.

Both Aiesha and Lakeesha are fairly representative of the girls who crossed my path. Samantha, a girl I also spent a fair amount of time getting to know, is less typical. Samantha, a white girl originally from Lee with two previous assault charges, was sent to New Directions for hitting another female youth over the head with a bottle—the other girl needed 19 stitches and almost lost an eye. Her resort to violence was more extreme than many of the girls I met. In her case, the role her mother played in shaping her use of violence was quite apparent. As previously noted, Samantha's mother, Melinda, burned Samantha with cigarette butts on a number of occasions. Melinda also had a long arrest record in her own right, including lots of assaults. It would be fair to say that, in Samantha's family, no distinction in norms was made with respect to males and females fighting. According to Samantha, her whole family at one time or another has been locked up, including her two sisters; two of the three boys had dealings with family court, as well. In fact, Samantha's older sister Karen (the oldest of the five children) was charged with aggravated assault as an adult when she was 17, given the severity of the altercation—Karen broke the girl's nose and collarbone as a result of repeatedly slamming her against the ground.

Samantha reports that, when she was seven or eight years old, her mother told her that if she did not defend herself against kids who picked on her, "she would beat her up herself"—a not uncommon exchange between mothers and daughters. Samantha must have realized from a young age that her mother meant business. Talking in a matter of fact way about "doing what she has to do," she gives a clear sense of a me-or-them sensibility:

> I can care less who gets hurt as long as it's not me. My mother said I better fight if someone threatens me. If I lose, she gonna understand, but if I bring home some problem without even trying to stand up for myself, she's gonna be on my case about why. I guess she don't want to be raising no punk. She wants me to be able to stand up strong. She also don't want to be having to fight my battles. She has enough things to deal with without that. She don't want to have to be chasing after me.

One can hear in this statement how the role norms usually associated with girls' socialization—passivity and providing nurture—were not just deemphasized in Samantha's case but were penalized. Moreover, common sense suggests that the lesson in aggression management given by Samantha's extremely violent maternal role model increased the likelihood that Samantha would transgress more typical gender norms associated with violence in an extreme way. Yet, while one can easily hear in Samantha's narrative how her mother helped to train her to be violent, again, it's also important to factor in how local social networks in Samantha's neighborhood reinforced those teachings and are implicated in Samantha's resort to violence. Clearly, Samantha was cautioned to defend herself against other children who very likely were receiving messages about fighting that, while perhaps different in degree, were similar in kind. Only if we start from a place where fighting is viewed as something that is broader than individual pathology is it possible to begin to understand both its makeup and its frequency.

While girls can inflict harm seemingly with abandon, and although they typically contend that they do not care whether what they do hurts someone else, in reality, many things they do and say contradict that assertion. Evidence that girls can take the perspective of the other is seen in their relationships with friends, a comment they make about a stray animal, or a sympathetic view that they take about the bad fortune of a sick relative who they believe to be a good person. Generally, it is not that a girl is without the psychological capacity to identify with or understand another person's situation or feelings, suggestive of a sociopathic personality; in most cases, the social situation surrounding violence in low-income communities like Melrose Park and Lee must be brought into the foreground to understand behavior.

In Samantha's case, the loss of empathy appeared more comprehensive than limited to her immediate adversaries. Again, Samantha does not represent the typical girl I followed. Her resort to violence should be thought of as falling at the far end of the spectrum and, importantly, being driven by deeper familial and personal issues than is the case for many other girls: Samantha experienced significant trauma during her developmental years, in keeping with a history of family violence and other dysfunction. More than any of the other girls I followed closely, Samantha appeared to have problems commonly associated with the diagnosis of an attachment disorder. Though she is more the exception to the rule, frequently both male and female youths who engage in violence, especially those who become known to the criminal justice system, are seen as psychologically damaged. While certain behaviors often accompany psychiatric diagnoses, behavior alone does not make a diagnosis. The wide range of personality traits that the girls I followed exhibit testify to this. The psychological makeup of the girls does not fit a single profile.

Needless to say, the three mothers discussed above bring personal differences to the table, which influence how they socialize their daughters to aggression. While each recognizes the need to prepare her daughter to live in a neighborhood where violence is all too common and in a larger society that will devalue her, each does so in her own way. And, at the same time that each wants her daughter to transcend the limitations of the immediate neighborhood, each understands the price of choosing not to socialize her daughter into an assertive posture, both verbally and physically, to "survive" the neighborhood. The balance of these two poles is something that mothers in Melrose Park and Lee have to constantly negotiate. Despite their differences, all the mothers I dealt with understood "the place" that violence had in their neighborhood and in her daughter's life. They understood that a blanket statement urging their children to repudiate violence and turn their back on fighting was not meaningful in the context of the world in which they lived. No doubt, were a mother to believe that her daughter simply just had to "say no" to violence, as the public service campaign of the 1980s under Nancy Reagan suggested, she would certainly opt for such a solution.[4]

As mentioned earlier, whereas sexual abuse is often cited as a major factor in why girls turn to violence, as is physical abuse, it is noteworthy that of the three mothers discussed above, only Samantha's mother is reported to have physically abused her daughter, and none of these three girls reported being victims of sexual abuse. While scholars of girls' violence have routinely put forth the argument, in Melrose Park and Lee, one cannot convincingly make the case that only, or primarily, girls who have been sexually or physically abused resort to engaging in physical violence. Similar to the deviance pathology argument, too large a percentage of the population of female youth in both neighborhoods engage in street fighting to understand their behavior as caused in large part, if not only, by such exploitation.

Mothers in Melrose Park and Lee typically do not encourage so-called feminine and dainty behavior. Moreover, in Melrose Park and Lee, engaging in physical violence does not necessarily cause an adolescent girl to be thought of as any less feminine than girls who do not fight. Rather, femininity as constructed by mainstream culture, while not rejected outright by low-income urban girls, is selectively appropriated alongside values that more closely fit their lives. However, while there is a considerable literature on how male youths in economically impoverished urban enclaves construct and affirm their masculinity through violence (Oliver,

1994; Bourgois, 1995; Anderson, 1999), relatively little has been written about how female youths in such neighborhoods who also engage in violence negotiate their femininity. It is as if the resort to violence automatically suggests a problem with gender role socialization and identification and undermines the assumptions underlying what it means to be a well-adjusted and genuine girl.

Interestingly, although girls in Melrose Park and Lee often assert themselves aggressively, they typically assume a traditional feminine role in their relations with boys. I observed girls routinely placing the interests of their boyfriends above their own, frequently catering to boys in a caretaking role, and spending a great deal of time on their appearance. For example, Lakeesha, with whom I hung out several nights a week in Melrose Park, carefully chose her outfits and applied her makeup before leaving the house. She and her friend Candace talked a great deal about how they were going to fix their hair and wanted to "look good" for their current romantic interest, which could change from week to week. Much of their extra money was spent on clothing and getting their hair done at the local beauty salon. The emphasis placed on outward appearance by girls who fight in low-income neighborhoods seemed quite characteristic of girls in their general age range. There was no indication that girls who readily gravitated toward fighting were any less self-conscious with their appearance than those who fought the least.

The preoccupation with appearance does not fade away even when girls know that they are going to fight. For instance, if time permits, a girl will remove her hair extensions so they do not get destroyed should her hair get pulled in a fight. In some cases, two girls on the brink of fighting will agree to meet at an appointed time so they can go home to change their clothes. In addition to the meticulous self-care Lakeesha is known for, she has a long list of war scores to her credit, some of which have left scars on her opponents. The identities of Lakeesha the adolescent girl interested in attracting boys and Lakeesha the fighter do not cancel out or oppose one another.

In sum, there is little evidence to suggest that girls who engage in fighting view themselves to be any less feminine for resorting to violence. Nor did anything I observed lead me to believe that boys necessarily perceived girls who fought to be any less feminine, either. As Allie, an attractive girl who is popular with boys, notes, "I can be cute yet still mess some girl up, if that's what I have to do." Allie apparently had no trouble finding boys who were interested in calling themselves her boyfriend. Indeed, I often found that boys took pride in the physical prowess of their girlfriends. Some boys would even come to watch if they knew that their girlfriend was going to fight. It is the girl who fights excessively who is more likely to be perceived as operating outside of appropriate gender expectations, not the girl who fights for the "right" reasons; we will see that this is true for a girl's mother, as well. Suffice it to say, from the perspective of the residents of Melrose Park and Lee, violence is something that can, and does, get meted out by both males and females.

Fighting Histories of Mothers

One must also look closely at the fighting history of girls' mothers, given the integral role that mothers play in the development of their daughters' use of violence. It is noteworthy that, of the mothers I spoke with directly or heard about indirectly over the course of my study, nearly everyone had a history of fighting when she was younger, ranging from just a few fights to a more regular frequency, and about one-third had yet to stop fighting altogether. Even those women who had not had a fight in several years left the possibility of fighting open if it was "necessary"— that is, if it came down to defending her family or someone she felt loyal to. The list of provocations that justified taking a situation to the level of a physical altercation might be longer, depending on the individual parent. Much had to do with the situation that presented itself. Over and over, I heard mothers say that, despite their best efforts, fighting or the threat of fighting was a medium that one sometimes had to communicate in. This was true even of the women who had not fought for a long time. Lakee-sha's mother, Fazia, explains:

> I've been on my own since I was 11. Used my body to take care of myself. I was in a foster home 'cause my mother wouldn't take me back. I was physically and sexually abused by relatives. I learned to be strong, strong-willed, strong-minded. Learned how to fight by getting beat up. No choice sometimes but to fight. Would fight with a weapon sometimes—a screwdriver. Not like it is now. You could talk your way out of it. It's different now. Whole block helped raise kids. Kids didn't disrespect their elders. Doesn't happen that way now. Generations have changed. Outside, kids are different people. They're a lot wilder today. Someone puts hands on your person, you

must protect yourself. Kids fight about the same things. Respect, that is, what they feel they deserve. Most of the young guys rather sell than have a job. Fast money. Look at it a certain way—to be known. There are drugs everywhere, everyone gets high. Me, I haven't had a fight in about 10–15 years, but I used to fight a lot before I became a Muslim. If you're a kid, you really have to be able to defend yourself at some point, not just talk a good game. Talking these days can only go so far without being able to put your fists where you mouth is.

The excerpt gives a sense of the adversity Fazia faced as a child and how she managed as best she could under those circumstances. Fazia certainly makes a connection between the trauma of her younger years and her subsequent use of violence as an adult. She identifies her use of violence as having instrumental value, in terms of both her psychological survival and her survival on the street. She suggests that it was through becoming "strong" (psychologically and physically) and a Muslim (spiritually) that she was able to eventually experience some measure of control in her turbulent life. The excerpt conveys that Fazia saw the resort to physical aggression as a first step in establishing a relatively peaceful existence in her community. Once she was able to feel more empowered both internally and externally, her need to dominate others on a physical level diminished.

It is generally not a disappointment to a girl if her mother fights, especially if the reasons for fighting are deemed necessary and proper. However, a girl typically takes a negative view of her mother's fighting if her mother was "high" when the altercation took place. It is one thing for a girl's mother to stand up for herself if she is put in a position where not to do so would suggest a failure of character and another thing if one's mother is out of control and acting like "she be a kid or something." For a mother to "act like a hood" was an embarrassment, whereas bold behavior teetering on recklessness by a girl was likely to be viewed by her peers as impressive.

Indeed, most of the mothers I spoke with (including Fazia) reported cutting back significantly on the extent to which they fought once they became pregnant with their first child. Along these lines, Cassie offers some insights regarding her mother, Estrella:

My mother was in a gang. Her friend died in her arms. She [her mother] tried to shoot her own mother. She was only in gang because her moms wouldn't take care of her. My mother really raised herself. Her mother was an alcoholic. We haven't seen her much over the last years. Someone killed my mother's father right after she was born. My moms had her son when she was 16, and then she stopped being in a gang. She was supposedly a pretty good fighter in her day, but she don't really do that stuff anymore. Now her kids fight [*laughing*].

Cassie's mother's story, while fraught with extreme violence, is not terribly uncommon. Historically, it is well known that gang life has been a refuge for urban youths in impoverished neighborhoods with troubled backgrounds—the lure being the sense of belonging, empowerment, and structure that it offers. Whereas gang presence on the street had significantly declined in Philadelphia in the 1990s—indeed, none of the girls I came in contact with were members of gangs—when Estrella was growing up, organized gangs were a major element in poor Philadelphia neighborhoods.[5] Therefore, not surprisingly, a number of the mothers of the girls I followed reported having some kind of involvement with gangs in their youth, although gang membership and affiliation in their day was largely male. Often the involvement of mothers was limited to being the girlfriend of a gang member rather than fighting themselves. While there were exceptions, even those exceptions were limited to street fighting or holding drugs for a boyfriend.

Adia's account of her mother's fighting history also supports the idea that females tend to gravitate away from street fighting once they became pregnant. In Adia's mother Angeline's case, the theme of gang life appears once again:

My mother and aunt hung together in a gang when they were coming up. They beat up people, I know 'cause she told me. My mother, she stopped fighting when she had kids. None of her sisters fight now. My mother no longer fights. She doesn't feel like she has to go that far, but I know that she would if it came down to protecting her family. But she ain't no low-life, and so she keeps out of that kind of trouble. She don't go looking for it, if you know what I mean. People pretty much know not to mess with her at this point. She gets a lot of respect from people.

Adia's excerpt is especially interesting with respect to the distinction she makes between mothers who fight and those who do not fight ("she ain't no low-life"). As noted above, while there is widespread acceptance of others fighting in situations where family safety or respect is seen as being challenged, or as a matter of loyalty, gratuitous fighting by mothers is looked down on. There is a social expectation that after females have children they will "grow up" and take care of their family. Thus, fighting pursued in the name of family well-being is seen as honorable, whereas fighting that is not connotes a lack of responsibility. Said another way, not all fighting by mothers is considered alike by the community. Just as perceptions about girls' fighting exists on a continuum, the very same can be said about the fighting in which girls' mothers engage.

In many ways, the world in which girls in Melrose Park and Lee are trying to find their way in today is not so different from the world of their mothers when their mothers were coming of age. Perhaps it is most accurate to say that the issue is one of degree. Most of the adults with whom I spoke felt that the "street" had become more dangerous for children, both male and female, and that the stakes and the rules had changed significantly. None of the parents I spoke with thought this was for the better. Most thought that the amount of fighting that girls engaged in today was far greater, and far more serious, with respect to degree. Tamika's mother, Ella, who was no stranger to fighting as a girl, tries to explain:

> Kids these days really can't get by without knowing how to defend themselves. Girls fought when I was coming up, but it's much worse now. It's not just kids who come out on the street but grown women. Down here [Melrose Park] is terrible. A lady brought her kids to fight just the other day. A lot of this fighting starts out being about boys or something ridiculous. Girls are gonna line up to fight you. I think that it's hard to be a kid today. Really hard. The terms of handling yourself are a lot more complicated with a lot more implications.

While Aiesha's mother, Ruthie, acknowledged that she did "a little fighting" as a teenager, in my many conversations with her, she emphasized that the use of weapons back then was much more of a rarity. Displaying great emotion in her voice, she told me that she had never felt the need to walk the streets carrying a knife like kids do today or to fight with a weapon—nor did she personally know anyone who did. She also described the street fighting of her day as being "fair" for the most part. She elaborates:

It was one to one. You had a problem with someone, you settled it, and then it was over. You didn't have to worry that anyone was going to come back with a gun. You didn't expect a girl to pull a knife on you or jump you when you weren't looking with five or six other girls. That's what you have to be expecting today. It's a whole different ball-game out there today. It's downright scary. Downright stupid. And it makes me really mad to think about it. The whole thing just don't make a lot of sense.

In contrast to Ruthie, who has not had a fight for several decades, Kia's mother, Terry, continues to this day to fight on a regular basis. Terry grew up in a single-parent household and was the youngest of four children. While she never was in trouble with the law, according to Kia, she was always on "the wild side." Kia explains that her mother had "a lot of prob-lems" when she was a teenager, and, in fact, Kia was sent to live with her grandmother for a few years after she was born while her mother "got her act together." It seems that Terry began using drugs shortly after she had Kia and has had a string of arrests for shoplifting related to her drug use. Kia describes her mother as having a short fuse and a big mouth. Kia appears to be at a real loss to explain why her mother continues in her ways, however. She also seems quite genuine when she says that she does not like it when her mother fights:

My mother just a few months ago got to arguing with someone from the neighborhood. I'm not sure what it was about, but she hit some-one with a stick and then pulled a knife. These kids were holding my mom back. The lady, she then came back with two others. My mother brought ten other people. My mother got hit on the head. The whole thing was a big mess. The cops came, but they didn't arrest no one because nobody really got hurt. Usually the cops won't bother unless the situation gets really messed up and way out of hand.

Unlike Kia's mother, the majority of the mothers of the girls I followed, including those whom I have mentioned and those whom I have not spo-ken about specifically, only fight under limited circumstances. Indeed, Shayleen says her mother, Gloria, only fights "when she has to," which means she stands up to anyone harassing her, but "is not out there" look-ing for a fight. The same goes for Tamika's mother, Ella. Though Ella had an extensive fighting history when she was growing up, since she stopped drinking a year ago, she reports rarely engaging in physical altercations. The only time Ella says she now gets involved in a fight is when someone "gets in her face" or if she has to stand behind her kids.

However, it is important to emphasize that what constitutes a threat differs from mother to mother. Fazia, Lakeesha's mother, puts it like this:

> Girls and women are more emotional. They get hyped. They don't want to calm down. It's just in them. It's who they are. So it doesn't take much for the words to go flying, and the fists can follow close behind unless you decide that you just ain't gonna live that way. It takes a while for a girl to get to the place where she is gonna give it up, but you can tell when a girl makes the decision 'cause she seems different. Things don't bother her like they did.

While mothers, for the most part, agreed that girls cannot avoid fighting at least some of the time, they were unanimous in their recognition of the tendency of girls to keep contentious situations going far longer than necessary. Mothers, to the contrary, seemed more ready to end contentious situations that turned physical once the immediate emotions tied to them dissipated. For most mothers, the need to employ judgment and maturity when assessing the "need" to fight was cited again and again. Clearly for most mothers, as they aged, their egos were less dependent on the sense of empowerment that fighting often delivered. They tell a similar story whereby discretion was exercised as a matter or strategic course and principle, and only when discretion failed was the possibility of physical confrontation brought into play.

Alliances and the Double-Generational Dynamic

As touched on previously, primarily with respect to peers, girls typically rely on a network of females to ensure their physical safety. However, mothers and female relatives are an important part of a girl's backup network, too. As briefly discussed in chapter 1, there are certain circumstances, including bringing a fight to a girl's doorstep (a major sign of disrespect) and when a one-on-one fight between two girls turns unfair (that is, when additional girls enter into the fight or weapons are introduced), that can elevate an altercation to a more-serious level where a girl's mother will jump in. With regard to the first matter—bringing a fight to a girl's doorstep—one's house is seen as being off limits to such confrontations. Often, when a fight comes to the household doorstep, it is made "unavoidable." It means that a girl, and, by association, her family, is being "called out." Even if that is not the intention of the female youth who approaches, a girl's mother typically views the situation as a threat or a challenge she will not tolerate. The mother is going to protect her house and her children, as well as the family's reputation to withstand confrontation. Similarly, no mother wants to be thought of as not protecting or standing by her daughter if her daughter is attacked under unequal conditions.

The "double-generational" dynamic, whereby mother and daughter fight alongside one another, is an important feature of fighting in Melrose Park and Lee, having no obvious parallel among boys and their fathers. Little if any scholarship has been devoted to the phenomenon. As Fazia, Lakeesha's mother, passionately notes:

> No hood gonna be coming up to my doorstep and menace me. You keep that junk on the street and out of my house. You come to my house, it's no longer between my daughter and that person. Now she gonna have to deal with me, and I ain't no little kid. That ain't no joke. A girl shouldn't be acting like no woman, and she shouldn't be going up to no one's door acting like she big and bad.

Under such conditions, it is accepted—indeed, even expected—that a mother will go out on the street with her daughter. Whereas a girl's loyalty to various peers will almost certainly undergo change over time, in some cases on a weekly basis, mothers tend to be permanently committed to "watching the backs" of their daughters. And while a mother obviously could not be expected to intervene in what she does not know about, it would be unusual for a mother to stay away when she knew that her daughter was outside fighting, especially if the fight was going on in front of her house.

Much of the time when a fight comes to a girl's doorstep, it is not brought there by just one other girl. Sometimes a girl will come with "her posse," either because she wants to up the ante or because she perceives the girl to have upped the ante on her. At other times, a girl's mother will accompany her daughter to another woman's doorstep because she perceives her daughter to be in danger and feels the fight needs to be raised to the level that includes mothers.

An example involving Lakeesha's mother, Fazia, is a case in point of a fight that unfolds along these lines. Though Fazia had managed to avoid fighting for many years, approximately a month after we had our first lengthy conversation about girls' violence and her own fighting history, she ended up fighting a 20-year-old woman who rang her doorbell. The woman came to her house to accuse Lakeesha of "messing" with her boy-friend. Incensed that the young woman brought the fight not even to the gate of her front yard but right up to her door, after a verbal exchange that apparently escalated, Fazia "got in her [the young woman's] face." The two began throwing punches, with Fazia reportedly getting the better of the other woman. But even before the first punch was thrown, accord-ing to bystanders, around 30 people, mostly women, surrounded them. Included in the group were neighbors who lived on the block, two friends who were visiting Lakeesha at the time, and people in cars who pulled over to get a better view of the spectacle. By the time the police came to break up the altercation, several additional fights had broken out among the many people who had gathered—the young woman had brought four or five associates with her to Fazia's door, and neighbors who knew the young woman, as she was from the area, also took up for her.

Given how large the crowd that gathered was, the police arrived fairly quickly on the scene. Even after the police told Fazia that they would arrest her if she did not stop fighting and go back into her house, she refused to. As discussed in chapter 6, often when females are given the chance to walk away from a situation to avoid arrest, unlike males, they will continue to argue and, according to police officers, give up the chance to end the incident without further problem. Fazia, admittedly prone to "pyrotechnics" if she "lets herself go down that road," was apparently too worked up to go inside. And since she would not go inside, the police arrested her and took her down to the station. Fazia was issued a cita-tion to appear in court two weeks later, as were several other females in the crowd; indeed, the situation got so out of hand that the police took more than ten females down to the station in a paddy wagon. At her court date, Fazia was ordered to attend an anger management class and to perform 20 hours of community service, which she agreed to. I could not help but wonder if my presence and my inquiry had in some way played a role in Fazia fighting after the decade-plus abstinence she had behind her.

Afterward, Fazia seemed to truly regret that she had let herself get pulled into the altercation and spoke about it at length when I accompanied her to her hearing. She realized that it was just "dumb stuff" and that she should have sent the girl on her way. Yet, on the other hand, she was still incensed that the young woman had the audacity to show up on the front steps of her house like she had. Fazia clearly had not put the incident behind her at the time of the hearing. Perhaps even more significant than the reaction that Fazia had on an emotional level was the practical matter of the woman having called attention to herself—getting "crazy" in front of Fazia's house made the situation a "show" for "everyone to see." Within the respect-driven ethos of the neighborhood, Fazia was pressed to make her response equally as public. The dispute escalated, and, after much verbal back and forth, it resulted in a slew of punches being thrown from both sides.

Lakeesha, in contrast, seemed to take pride in how "crazy" her mother had gotten. She said, with a wide grin on her face: "My mother has a good bout game [she boxes well]." Rather than being humiliated by her mother's fighting, her mother's fighting was big news in Lakeesha's school the next day, and, as a result of it, Lakeesha gained minor celebrity status for a short time. Although there was some degree of tension between students who supported Lakeesha and those who were more allied with the young woman, nothing more came of it.

It is just as important to address the fact that mothers are stalwart in not intervening under certain circumstances, too. A mother's involvement is typically grounded not in preventing her daughter from fighting but in making sure a fight goes down "on the up and up." Frequently, a mother will just stand by while her daughter fights it out just to make sure "no one gets in it." Typically, a mother will only jump in when several girls start fighting at once or, on the rare occasion, when she cannot break up a fair fight in which her daughter is being badly beaten up. A mother might also jump in if she perceives the mother of the girl fighting her daughter to disrespect her or to directly challenge her. Fazia speaks to the situation:

> I don't usually get in her business, but if the fight isn't gonna come down fair, I can't not get involved. Anything can happen out there, and you have to let people know you gonna protect your kid. It has a lot more to do with making your intentions known than anything else. It usually doesn't come down to getting involved, just showing that you will if you have to.

As we have seen, a girl's mother usually sees encouraging her daughter to learn how to protect herself as the best way to protect her daughter; yet, she also knows how dangerous the streets are and is not without worry about a fight careening out of control. One can hear the tension in Fazia's words as she talks about when to and when not to get involved:

> In some sense it's an art. Figuring out when to let your kid settle their own problems and when to get involved. Around here it's not like other neighborhoods where if you're wrong, you just chalk it up to experience and do better the next time. I mean, it's not like every fight is gonna lead to your kid getting killed, but you miss a situation that is serious trouble and you got some serious trouble. So you gotta always be smart. You gotta always take precautions. There ain't no fooling around out here.

This said, during my fieldwork, I had, on several occasions, seen a mother stop an onlooker from breaking up a fight, even when her daughter was not winning. Indeed, adults in Melrose Park and Lee recognize that, when a girl fights, she is practicing standing up for herself and typically "allow" a fight to continue. Fights that take place on school grounds do not typically last as long because school personnel intervene quickly, though the altercation that starts in school often gets finished after the end of the school day.

In short, mothers have a steadfast identification and commitment to their daughters' safety. Paradoxically, this commitment can act to encourage a girl to escalate a violent situation, as many a girl knows that she is virtually assured of additional reinforcements. Common sense dictates that a girl who does not feel secure in her backup is more likely to avoid the possibility of a fight escalating whenever possible, if for no other reason than that her chances of prevailing are lessened. The surer a girl is that she can rise to the occasion if her opponent raises the stakes, the more confident she will be in putting forth the message that she is "ready."

The identification and commitment goes both ways. In most cases, no matter how angry a girl may be at her mother for past transgressions, she will also defend her. As Samantha, the youth whose mother had burned her with cigarette butts when she was younger, passionately comments:

If you say something about my father, I never fight over him. He gives me money. But you can't say anything about my moms. If it weren't for my moms, I wouldn't be here. Your mom is your highest, she raised you. Especially, with no father around. She break her back for you. You have to respect her for that, no matter anything else. I be there for her if she need it. I think my mother know that about me, no matter what goes down between us, and I know that about her, no matter what.

Why the double-generational dynamic in which mothers fight alongside their daughters has no corresponding parallel to boys and their fathers has not been carefully studied; however, the reasons are not so difficult to fathom. In the first place, there are fewer fathers who live with or stay in steady contact with their sons. Some have minimal ties at best, and many are in prison. Moreover, it may be that a boy whose uncles or brothers came to his side would be seen as unable to fight his own battles, thus undermining the boy's stature rather than strengthening it. The same conclusion is not typically drawn if a girl's mother comes to her daughter's defense. Rather, when males fight alongside each other outside of the structure of a gang, it is usually a small group of peers who "run" together. In my travels, I did not see or hear of fights where more than four or five male youths fought it out. The fights were typically one on one, unless they were in some way gang related.

On ride-alongs with police, the phenomenon of mother/daughter and female group fighting was apparent. On numerous occasions, I observed encounters where between 20 and 30 females gathered in relation to a fight. In one instance, the police were called back three times—the first two times, the police just broke the altercation up and issued warnings. However, the third time they came back, they handcuffed a mother, her daughter, an aunt, and a cousin and took them away in the police wagon. Several other women were taken away separately in squad cars. Whereas not all of the women who gathered actually became physical, those who did not were yelling and maintained a verbal presence making taunts to the other side and egging on those who became physically involved. Again Sergeant Palazzio notes:

> Girls and women are more emotional. They get hyped. They don't want to calm down. They have to mouth off. Too much pride to back down. Even when you tell them you're going to take them in, they

just keep at you. My female officers tell me that they'd rather deal with breaking up guys' fights any day. Once a girl [or any female] starts up, it takes a lot more to get her to back down. It's a whole lot more trouble. It doesn't have to be that way, but that's how it is a lot of the time. It's hard to talk sense into a female who thinks she's been treated badly whether in reality she has been or not.

6

Culture and
Neighborhood Institutions

*I don't think that most teachers really care about kids. Most
kids in my school gonna tell you that, that is if they're being
honest. It don't matter to me what they think about me because
it shouldn't be like that. It's not all teachers that are concerned
about collecting their paycheck, but most of them are.*

—Samantha, a 14-year-old girl

*Most kids come to school needing a lot more than instruc-
tion in math and reading. They're dealing with so many
things, problems at home, there are drugs all around them,
it's amazing that we can do much teaching at all. We're just
not relevant, given what they have to face every day. The attitude that comes through the door is what has to be addressed
before anything else can happen. But it's the rare kid who can
leave his or her attitude at the door and then pick it up at 3
PM to face the rest of his or her day.*

—Mr. Gordon, a teacher at New Directions
alternative high school

It is not only one's mother, other family members, or peers that shape
a girl's relationship to violence. The institutional infrastructure of the
community, comprised by its schools, housing, police force, criminal justice system, and the configuration of its commercial economy, among
other institutions, plays an important role in the production and reproduction of violent events in a given neighborhood or in the limiting of
such events, too. Clearly, neighborhoods are places where people share

more than just geography. They are places where people are likely to share some degree of cultural identity, cultural language, social perceptions, and interests. Neighborhood institutions, which are the building blocks for a healthy local economy and the foundation on which strong communities rest, are vital to informing what the outlook of a community is. For example, the quality of the education system and other public institutions of a neighborhood quickly suggest to residents whether their neighborhood has been left behind or is one of promise and opportunity. In neighborhoods where social institutions do not function to sufficiently maintain faith in the possibility of a better future, the future for many residents grows much dimmer—a phenomenon I readily observed in Melrose Park and Lee. As Cornel West (1993) put it, in neighborhoods where social institutions are "depressed," so are the inhabitants who depend on them for their livelihood and for their well-being.

Indeed, it is not only the condition of the housing stock that becomes eroded when houses fall into disrepair or simply disappear. Perhaps even more important, the community cohesion of a neighborhood suffers (Sampson et al., 1997). To suggest this is not meant to imply that all the residents of a neighborhood have become disconnected from their fellow counterparts, only that the sense of community among residents in a given neighborhood gets broken down in important ways—public space and public activities are compromised by the "street" being viewed as unsafe. The diminution of such a feeling has significant implications for the incidence of violence in that, as the sense of one's connection to others lessens, the barriers against the discharge of aggressive impulses frequently are also lowered (Sampson et al., 1997; Jacob, 2006). Similarly, the less that one feels that there is to preserve materially, the greater the chances are that the constraints against destructiveness will be lessened, as well.

In addition to the observation noted above, also relevant to this discussion, West (1993) has persuasively argued that culture is as much a "structure" as the economy and politics are. When he refers to culture as a structure, however, West is not just referring to the network of roles and functions that typically comprise an institution but, rather, to a structure of feeling, values, and ideas that gets encoded into the everyday social life of a community and to which social groups, as active agents, then negotiate. As an institution, culture provides the system of collective norms by which a community organizes the world and gives meaning to events and behaviors. As such, institutions play a role in socializing, teaching, and educating the young. In a loosely parallel way, neighborhoods shape girls' attitudes, beliefs, and values, similar to how parents, extended family, and peers do. It would be fair to say that in Melrose Park and Lee, a girl's feelings, values, ideas, and practices associated with violence are in dialogical relationship to a wide range of institutions. Major institutions relate to and view the populations that they serve in collective and stereotypical ways, rather than individualized ones. One more deeply comes to understand what it means for a girl to engage in violence through attempting to make sense of how girls characteristically are perceived by neighborhood institutions that importantly influence their lives and how, over time, girls themselves come to view those institutions.

As touched on earlier, there is a generalized feeling among residents of Melrose Park and Lee of being marginalized by mainstream culture. The African American and Hispanic girls with whom I spoke typically saw themselves as closed out of white, middle-class America and abandoned by the failing institutions meant to serve them. Barring a few exceptions, they perceived the authorities in their lives—their teachers, potential neighborhood employers, and the police—as viewing them negatively or, in a word, as being "ghetto," a word that suggests the intrinsic lack of their cultural or personal value. While girls in Melrose Park and Lee are often quick to refer to themselves as ghetto, the term in their hands possesses a different connotation: in addition to referencing a certain "style" (loudness, kind of dress, etc), "ghetto" stands for doing things against mainstream culture "their way." On a surface level, it means rejecting mainstream values as anything they would be interested in.

This is not to say that the girls are single-minded about perceiving all of the professionals in their lives as uncaring, but rather, that if a professional genuinely takes an interest in them, it is seen as being out of the ordinary. Girls certainly reported having a favorite teacher, a "good" probation office, or a lawyer at Legal Aid who really cared about what happened to them, but such relationships were the exception rather than the rule. However, for most girls, the stories laced with disappointment are the ones that get repeated again and again and function as the organizing subtext of a girl's experience at school.

Education

Whether at Franklin High, at New Directions, at Paulson, or at Compton-Taylor, the threat of violence breaking out on school grounds constitutes a major preoccupation of school personnel, resulting in school corridors being transformed into tightly controlled spaces. Time and time again, I observed the military-like paradigm that John Devine (1996) describes in his book *Maximum Security: The Culture of Violence in Inner-City Schools*, particularly how the school day is organized around practices of keeping order rather than imparting knowledge and how the expectation that order will turn to disorder shapes the sequence of the school day. As Devine points out, school budgets for educational programs and resources are typically slashed in inner-city schools, while money allocated for surveillance (i.e., guards, metal detectors, and cameras) continues to multiply.[1] Although an institution dedicated to the training of the mind, it can seem all too frequently that the priority becomes less educational and more custodial in nature. This seemed to be the case, particularly in the alternative school classrooms that I spent time in, regardless of the recent national emphasis on standardized testing and greater accountability requirements.

Indeed, alternative high schools rarely meet academic goals, given the nature of the population they serve and because graduation in four years is not relevant for many students who attend. If anything, the No Child Left Behind Act of 2001 has put more pressure on these schools. Although required by law to place children in failing schools into ones that perform better, in the 2005–2006 school year, of the 185,000 entitled to transfer, only 3,000 actually did so. In reality, there are insufficient openings to accommodate the need.

While I found security arrangements to differ between the mainstream and range of alternative schools in which I spent time, metal detectors and body searches were standard practice in all of them. In both types of schools, hall monitors acted as gatekeepers at strategic points on every floor, though security practices were more obvious in the alternative schools. For example, while youths at Franklin were searched before they entered the building, the youths at Paulson and New Directions, in addition to being searched, were not permitted to carry book bags with them into their classrooms. School authorities at these latter-mentioned schools were particularly concerned that their students might try to smuggle a weapon into the building, so personal possessions were confiscated at the front door and returned at the end of the school day. If a student needed an object from his or her book bag during the day, he or she would have to be accompanied by school personnel to get it. Despite the elaborate measures, some weapons, though clearly fewer than might otherwise have gotten through, still escaped detection.

In all of the schools in which I spent time, it was apparent that a student's comings and goings were under surveillance, and security practices were designed to meet safety guidelines set out in advance. Security guards and other staff members, including administrators and deans, carry walkie-talkies. On several occasions, I observed teachers using their cell phone to contact security personnel or the main office when trouble seemed to be looming. While the focus on security is an attempt to promote safety, students at the same time are also given the message that violence or something "bad" is expected of them. Beyond that larger apparent expectation, of course, the receipt of the message for a particular girl is individual. Adia, who is unique among her peers in her ability to maintain her future orientation and her clarity of what she wants to do, comments as follows:

> If you treat kids like they're a "hood" or something, they gonna feel like it don't matter how they act. These teachers here don't really know anything about me. I'm just gonna go about my business and get out of here as fast as possible because I know what I want to do with my life, so what they say to me don't really matter. I'm gonna be a funeral director someday and run a funeral parlor. I'm gonna own my own business.

While security arrangements acted to limit the number of weapons entering the building, they were less effective in controlling physical confrontations between students, which remained a major management issue, again, often at the expense of educating students. The same degree of vigilance was not similarly apparent when it came to teaching students. As long as a youngster was not overtly disruptive, his or her lack of participation generally went unchallenged. Most of the students in the schools I passed through appeared to have disengaged from learning a long time ago. At Paulson, for instance, it was typical to find half the students in a given classroom with their heads down on their desks while the teacher completed the lesson. The students who were "resting" were pretty much evenly split down the middle between males and females. Teachers would reach out initially, but when their efforts met no success after a while, a youth would for the most part be left alone.

When asked why they "slept" in class, girls offered a range of reasons, with "the work is boring" and "I was out late last night" being the most common. Sometimes girls simply questioned the importance a particular subject like algebra had for their future. As Kia put it, "I be doing all that work and not be using it." Even more to the point, most of the girls I came in contact with saw themselves as having limited horizons in the world of school and seemed to be investing their energies accordingly. Disturbing a girl once she decided to sleep sometimes resulted in a tense exchange between girl and teacher or the girl sitting up to make a faint effort. While not the policy of all teachers, most had reached a point of not pressuring students as long as they did not cause trouble. This allowed those students who wanted to participate to do so at the same time that it allowed the nonparticipating students to get credit for attendance. Many of the girls with whom I spoke said they only attended to avoid getting into more trouble with parents, probation officers, or someone in the system who had jurisdiction over them. At other times, girls engaged in doing their work might play around in the classroom. The atmosphere of the classrooms that I spent time in, especially in alternative schools, often seemed overly chaotic or overly subdued with little activity.[2]

This does not mean that girls did not have aspirations, though typically their aspirations were poorly organized. When I asked Manuela what she wanted to be when she grew up, she said "maybe a lawyer or a hair dresser." But as I pressed her to provide me with more details—for instance, what it took to get admitted to law school—her abstracted vision of entering the legal profession began to crumble. She seemed to recognize on some level that she lacked the necessary drive or resources to do all that was necessary to actually embark on such a demanding career path. Manuela's words convey the uncertainty:

> I ain't gonna go to all that school. That's gonna be too much. I'm gonna try to get a job bagging groceries this summer, but so far no luck. I've been worrying about it too much. I know I can make it. If I don't get a job at the grocery store, maybe I'm gonna look at the beauty parlor down my block. It gonna work out some way, I just know it. I'm not too worried about it.

Though Manuela's idea of success was not wholly divorced from mainstream values (being a lawyer), one can hear in the preceding excerpt how she vacillates between the psychological stances of trying and giving up. It seems that as long as she keeps alive the possibility of "making it," she does not have to directly face the anger and sense of humiliation associated with having limited career chances and economic possibilities. The ghetto attitude she displays and the street fighting in which she engages serve as an immediate way to feel important and to minimize any worry that she might have about her future. Each time Manuela hits a roadblock in her thinking, she reassures herself by raising the idea of another possibility without ever really weighing her actual prospects or feelings on the matter. At no time does she take stock of her prospects and think through her options. While the average youngster Manuela's age cannot be expected to know exactly how they will proceed along their career path, Manuela seemed unaware of what the requirements even were to embark in that direction.

Teachers in my study were willing to share their views and indeed were helpful in providing a window on their students' educational merit and sense of worth, as well as the range of attitudes that they as educational professionals held toward their students. When Mr. Gordon, a teacher at New Directions, was asked why kids do not invest more in their schoolwork, he said:

> What kids think of themselves has a lot to do with why they don't learn. They tune in to what they need in their neighborhoods. They're smart. But what they're interested in is based on what they need. They're not going outside the neighborhood. So it's a big challenge to teach them anything that doesn't have a direct application to their lives. They just don't see the relevance. It has to have immediate application for kids to want to give it their attention.

As Mr. Cuomo, a learning specialist who has worked at Paulson for nearly five years, notes:

> Most kids just don't care. . . . There are no consequences with this program. Kids perceive themselves as ghetto because institutions see them that way. They're going to school for bad kids. They learn to act that way. It wasn't that way at first. Wearing a shirt that says "Paulson" on it is a problem. The shirt labels them. It helps security to identify kids. When cops see them, pull them over, they won't look at them as kids but adults. It's a set up from the minute that they start in one of these programs, but there just isn't any other place for them. It's really a mess. It's like this vicious circle. Once you're in, it takes a

lot of focus to work your way out of it. And while some kids have that focus, at lot of them don't. A kid can come in with more focus than he or she leaves with. It all depends who the kid ends up associating with and if he or she connects to something or someone that is positive. Just one important person can make a difference for a kid.

Exhibiting the anger and alienation that many poor urban girls experience on a daily basis, Tamika, who seems irritated about a wide range of things, was quick to assert the following:

If a teacher gonna automatically think I'm stupid 'cause of the way I walk or talk—fuck her. I got nothing to say to her. She just be wasting her time trying to get me to pay attention and stuff like that. I ain't gonna listen to nobody like that. You don't respect me, then why am I gonna respect you? Forget that.

In Tamika's comment, one can clearly hear the relentless experience of being measured short. She would aptly be described as a girl who has a chip on her shoulder.[3] One gets the sense that Tamika rejects the teacher well in advance of being devalued herself. In effect, Tamika can only maintain her pride by separating herself from the institution of education and adopting an identity in opposition to it (Spencer et al., 2001); thus, whatever interest in learning she might have is likely to be suppressed. To learn, Tamika would have to admit to herself that she wanted to "get something" out of school. Revealing her hope as well as her need for remediation would likely cause her to feel too psychologically vulnerable. However, most of the girls I followed, who presented as being far less angry than Tamika, also saw their teachers as not really caring about their futures. Adia, a less-angry girl, offers a similar impression about the lack of concern that school personnel have for students:

I didn't want to go to class. I got kicked out of Franklin, so that's how I ended up here [New Directions]. I fought too much. Hung out with girls. Fought too much. Smoked all day. Weed. Cigarettes. At Franklin they don't care. You just walk in and out. I would cuss the teacher out. I haven't learned nothing at this place [New Directions]. Mr. Gordon, he my nigger though. He cares about kids, not like most teachers. He ok with me. I know that some other kids think that he's too strict, but he ok with me. He cares about the kids here.

Although Adia realizes the connection between her behavior (cursing at teachers and fighting) and getting in trouble in school, she does little if anything to change her behavior, as she sees school as a place where she "learn[s] nothing." She feels that school personnel have invested little in her, and she therefore makes no apologies for her behavior. While a teacher's concern is not a silver bullet, I did find that in classrooms where teachers were seen as caring about their student's individual needs and trying to make kids understand, there was a meaningful difference in how at least some girls applied themselves. Indeed, research supports the connection between engagement, achievement, and school behavior (Appleton et al., 2008): when teachers are viewed as having a greater investment in at-risk students, their performance is significantly affected in a positive way.[4]

Girls in Melrose Park and Lee are quick to blame teachers and school personnel for their academic problems and, in most cases, do not go the extra step to voluntarily reflect on how they view their own abilities. This said, if asked directly, most girls were aware of their academic difficulties. Cassie asserted:

> It's not my fault. I give it a try but I ain't understanding it or something. I don't know how to do these problems [math], so I just put my head down on the desk. They make me sleepy. I think if the work was more interesting, then I'd be able to stay awake more. When I like something, I guess I do better at it.

In this excerpt, Cassie goes from feeling inadequate to giving up to changing the subject by focusing on another reason for the problem. In the end, it is too uncomfortable for her to think for very long about how her own academic difficulties make her feel, so she offers another reason for her poor performance: not enough sleep. Truth be told, once girls in Melrose Park and Lee get to the point where they have fallen behind in school, the odds of them getting the help they need are decidedly against them. Moreover, in the cultural context in which they find themselves, learning is devalued and youths tend to collectively feed off each other's negative attitude about school, making an interest in learning something one feels one must hide. The vicious cycle of devaluation and withdrawal that characterizes many a youngster's educational experience in Melrose Park and Lee fits the classic picture of ghetto schooling that Jean Anyon (1997) and other scholars have poignantly written about.[5]

Many girls are further embarrassed because they have been placed at an alternative school, which makes caring about learning even more uncomfortable. Mr. Griffin, a serious, no-nonsense type of a person and a favorite and respected teacher of many kids at Paulson, speaks to this last point:

> Coming to an alternative school labels them. How it plays out depends. They are labeled to the outside world as bad kids. Being kicked out of the neighborhood. Has a lot to do with self-esteem. You know I see that some of these kids are really trying. But when they don't get it fast, a lot of them can't imagine that if they keep at it that they're going to get it. And once they are far behind, it's hard to give them all the time that they need to catch up in a meaningful way. So they just beat out time until they either get in more trouble and are removed or push through to the next class or grade before too many hackles get raised. I think we're doing most of these kids a disservice, but nobody seems to know what to do with them because their problems are so vast.

In the course of my work I found that even when teachers and school personnel were sympathetic to kids, they often were not well trained. Many teachers at Paulson, New Directions, and Compton-Taylor had little previous experience working in school settings; some did not have any degree in education at all, although many were actively engaged in pursuing some type of certification. There was also a high turnover among staff, given the low pay and probable burnout. Again, not surprisingly, it was the teachers who were both experienced and specifically devoted to working with inner-city youths who seemed to garner the most favorable response from them.[6]

It is in this context where girls for the most part feel little investment in school and perceive themselves to be devalued by school authorities that much fighting is planned out or breaks out. Schools end up being a meeting ground for youths to confer with one another about peer issues, which developmentally has primacy in their lives. It is frequently at school that the gossip that drives fights gets worked and reworked, with the range of circumstances that commonly provoke fights never being in short-supply. As Tamika describes:

> See someone speaking to the guy you're talking to, and it burns you up. You sit there all day thinking how you're gonna take care of that

bitch. Shit, it damn hard to wait 'cause you gotta stay right where you are until later when you can settle the matter in your own way. Once you're outside [of the school], it's a whole different matter. Sometimes girls they act big when they in school, but then they don't talk the same way when you see them outside because they know that they have to live up to how tough they be talking.

Fights that occur on site are usually the result of a spontaneous dispute over a perceived slight and often "go down" in the hallway. These same corridors are where information gets communicated about fights that have been broken up and will be continued when school lets out. It should be noted that at the schools in which I spent time, girls fought at least as much as boys. This is because boys, unlike girls, are less likely to fight over small slights, given the greater chance that an opponent might produce a gun—if not immediately, then at a later point in time. Both male and female youths were unanimous is confirming this observation.

However, without fail, school personnel uniformly viewed girls as being "tougher to handle" than boys. For now, suffice it to say that, at all the schools at which I spent time, girls' fights were deemed harder to break up, given the intensity with which girls "went at each other." Indeed, the word "intensity" was commonly used to refer to girls. Mr. Martin, the vice principal of Paulson, explains:

> The hardest thing is to keep a girl in her seat. They keep things going. They cross boundaries more. When girls get mad, they really lose it. Reasoning can only go so far if a girl gets her mind fixed about something. A lot of the time, you just have to wait it out and see if you can talk to her afterward. Usually that works a lot better. It's not that you can't talk to a girl, it's just finding the right way to approach her.

Mr. Gordon echoes the same sentiment as Mr. Martin but expands his comments further. Rather than simply being critical of the girls, he conveys an appreciation for the degree of competition that gets raised among them:

> About 80% of girls in my class fight. Girls are more far more dangerous than boys. They will cut you, stab you. Do what it takes to bring you down. Boys get that way, but it's not normal. Girls will do their best to hurt you. They will pull out every stop to get you. Throw

chairs, stab you with pencils, call you bad names; they will degrade each other. First thing they call each other is "bitch." Girls who stay out of fights establish respect. They let things go. But it's a balancing act because they also can't be seen as being scared to fight. We tell kids all the time not to fight and to use talking to settle situations, but if certain kids won't play by those same rules, then the case you're making against fighting falls apart.

Mr. Lawrence, a teaching manager at New Directions, specifically makes a connection between girls' academic weaknesses, their resort to fighting, and the larger context that influences their fighting:

A lot of girls try to deal with their educational flaws by being bad. Girls are harder to reason with than boys. They will argue. Most want attention. They want different attention than the boys. For boys, things aren't as deep. Words aren't a part of it. The boy just is going to earn his respect by fighting it out, and then it's usually over unless something goes down really wrong or if it's gang related. You don't see the same fight be fought over and over again by boys. When the fight is done, for the most part it's usually over.

Ms. Lafeyette, a behavioral specialist at Franklin, reinforces the view held by many that girls have more "issues" than boys:

Girls have a lot of issues. There are some services in school we offer, but they are not available to all girls. I think that they should be. A lot of girls have issues from home, mental health issues, traumatic issues of the past, neglected or abused in one way or another. Not necessarily by parents. There are a lot of things going on with girls. Makes it difficult to teach them. Much harder than boys. Maybe it would be better for girls to be in an all-girls environment. This way, they could get the attention that they need and not have things become more complicated when boys, on top of everything else, enter into the picture. When you add boys into the equation, the situation becomes exponentially more complicated with girls.

Clearly, however, at the schools I spent time in, personnel all too often played a role in exacerbating altercations by the way in which they intervened. When cursed out or otherwise challenged by students, security guards often became belligerent themselves. They would frequently restrain a youth before he or she became physically aggressive, intensifying the youth's sense of anger and frustration. Mr. Martin's comments with regard to the training and expertise of security personnel are illustrative on this score:

> School security people have to be really smart with girls. But sometimes they're just a little older than the kids are. They're usually from the same neighborhood. So sometimes they just grab kids, which causes situations to escalate. It's really institutionalized racism, you know, paying staff $6 and $7 an hour. I don't know what people think is going to happen when things from the get-go are set up like this [*he lets out a big sigh*]. And then the school is blamed because the trouble that occurs comes down during the school day on school property. The whole thing is crazy. What is wrong with the situation is larger than the kids, larger than the school. We need to make some significant changes in the way we run schools in inner cities if we expect things to really change in any significant sense.

Although youngsters in inner cities are often labeled as intellectually impaired based on their school performance, there is no yardstick that measures their intelligence in other arenas—in particular, their social intelligence with respect to reading their surroundings. Academic tests do not capture or credit the social skills intelligence and emotional intelligence that many of the youths I spent time with possessed. Unfortunately, institutional neglect (in the realm of education) interacting with personal disaffection renders many youths unlikely to use school to obtain a secure future. Said another way, on some level, the girls I followed were well aware of how behind they were academically and thus psychologically defended themselves against feeling humiliated by "opting out." Thus, for many of these girls, the attitudes, beliefs, and norms associated with doing well academically were unlikely to surface in the school setting.

The Juvenile Justice System

Several authors have noted the critical need to consider the juvenile justice system itself as a process structuring violent girls' lives (Chesney-Lind, 1997; Baskin and Sommers, 1997; Miller, 2001). In fact, we know relatively little about how the criminal justice system "constructs" girls as agents of aggression, not only with regard to the way in which girls are viewed by the system but also with respect to how a girl's self-construction is effected as a result of how they are viewed. Over the course of the past two decades, the way in which the criminal justice system has dealt with female youth offenders has also markedly changed.[7] As Judge Tessler, one of the judges I interviewed, who sits on the bench at Philadelphia Juvenile Court, was quick to note:

> We used to think of serious violent crime as being committed only by males. We see more girls than ever before. Mostly assaults. Before, girls' homicides were of infants in bathrooms. But girls are committing more of a scope of violent crime than before. I don't think that things are going to change for the better any time soon. It's my sense that we're going to see more girls coming into the system and with charges that have been historically reserved for boys. We're witnessing an important trend with respect to delinquency in this country and how it is dealt with.

With regard to the issue of prosecution, she continues:

> Charging youths as adults is a mistake. Children don't belong in the adult system. The mental health side of the law is what we need to have at our discretion. The old system was better. You also have a lot of girls now who are coming into the system, and there is little out there in terms of programs for them. I think that will change as the number of girls continues to rise. But it's going to take a while for the system to catch up, and the girls that are in the system before that happens will bear the burden of it. The question is how long is it going to take us to learn the lessons that we need to learn? The court system can do better for families and kids than it is currently doing.

In reality, over 85% of the youth cases that are filed directly to adult court are transferred back to juvenile court after a dispositional hearing.[8] Yet applying the full weight of the law to certain acts of violence by youth has gone far toward institutionalizing a view of youths as being of a different "breed" than their predecessors. John DiIulio (1995) coined the term "super-predator" to describe this "new" type of juvenile who is highly resistant to rehabilitation. Fraught with alarming implications and imagery that could easily be manipulated to inspire fear, the term was quickly embraced by the media in the mid 1990s. Many observers charged that the term had racist connotations in that it was disproportionately invoked in situations where minority youths were alleged to have committed serious violent acts.

While the specter of youth-as-super-predator was primarily associated with male youths, the effect of this revisionist view had great significance for girls. Girls' violent behavior had historically been minimized by the juvenile justice system. The zero-tolerance approach adopted by the criminal justice system in response to the increased incidence of youth violence in the late 1980s and early 1990s ushered in a less-chivalrous attitude toward the processing of female juvenile delinquency cases.[9] Judge Garrett, who also sits on the bench in Philadelphia Juvenile Court, weighs in on this point:

My hands are tied in some ways. There are more spots [in treatment programs] for males than females. Anything left over you give to girls. We're dealing with a lot of damaged kids. Society has failed these kids but doesn't forgive a kid for creating another victim. Just because you've been shuffled around in the system doesn't excuse you in the eyes of the law. Money is green self-esteem for these kids. We're seeing a lot more girls than we ever did before. To tell you the truth, I don't think we know what to do with them, and even if we did, we don't yet have the facilities in place to direct them to. It's a shame because these girls need help now, not in a few years. They need help today.

Lana, a probation officer with several years on the job, notes:

I've never seen a girl that was a big seller. Mostly they're brought in for aggravated assault. Girls, they tend to take everything to an extreme. They have more anger issues, anger at the world. A chip on their shoulder. I have a harder time communicating with them than with boys. Not sure why. More issues, pregnancy, and promiscuity, problems in the family—boys have less family problems. Girls have more mental health issues. I've been doing this for a while, and it's always been this way. We saw fewer girls in the system before, but when we saw them it was the same way.

She continues:

> I would rather have ten boys than one girl. Girls have an attitude: "You gonna give me my bus money or what" [*imitating a girl*]. They're more consuming. More issues to talk about. Even when they commit violence, girls are still feminine, still attached to males . . . they still continue to be secondary to males. Violence is its own thing. You have a lot more things going on with a girl. It's always a lot more complicated. That's just the way it is.

One must wonder what causes Lana to perceive female youths as having "more issues" than their male counterparts, though it is not just Lana who holds this view. The notion that males who fight are "rational" not "emotional," even when they use guns, is pervasive among juvenile justice personnel, just as it was with education personnel. Even though male youths often inflict greater harm than female youths, they still are typically viewed as being less angry. And despite the fact that male youths sell and consume drugs more often than female youths, more readily gravitate toward weapon use, and typically have relationships going with several girls at once, they are still seen as having fewer mental health problems than girls. Nor are they characterized as being promiscuous, as a girl who moves from partner to partner would be. Moreover, boys are seen as having fewer problems, even though male and female youths are reared in the same neighborhood in which poverty and its vicissitudes touch the lives of both. Yet, while it is no doubt true that girls present with a lot of attitude, the psychological factors that drive boys to commit violence are more complicated than is often acknowledged. It is too simple to leave it to the commonplace notion that "boys will be boys" or that boys are more aggressive. Personal factors weigh heavy in the lives of certain boys where violence is concerned and need to be factored in accordingly.

The differential perception of male and female youth violence has a paradoxical expression on the bench and in other levels of the criminal justice system. While the resort to violence by female youths is typically not perceived as being as serious as male youths, at the same time, female youths are viewed as being more psychologically unstable than their male counterparts. In some cases, this results in a girl receiving a more-treatment-oriented disposition. However, since there are relatively few treatment program slots for females, ironically, a girl often cannot get the help that she is deemed to need and ends up in a program where she receives limited services. Mental health and chemical dependency programs are in serious short supply for female youths, as are dual diagnosis spots in treatment facilities (Chesney-Lind et al., 2002). Though only a few, some studies provide evidence that increasing access to basic and specialized treatment programs with a special emphasis on the needs of female youths, including a range of services when girls are released back to the community, would go a long way to reduce recidivism and re-arrest rates.[10]

The following excerpt by Judge Rutter, who recently retired from the bench, well illustrates this position:

> It's different between girls and boys. Girls can retreat. There is no free ride for a boy. He has to show his mettle. Philly is a matriarchal society. To protect her young ones, a mother will go along to assure that her daughter doesn't get her face cut. Nothing a man can do about that. You're not going to stop a mother from going out on the street to protect her daughters. No matter what you say or do. She sees what she's doing as taking care of her kid, and she will risk what she has to risk to do that.

He continues:

> There is a pecking order among these girls. That's everything. If a girl violates the pecking order, there is going to be a problem. Every girl in a pack will assault the girl who violates the pecking order. If a girl asserts her right, other girls will support her choice. A girl can manipulate the situation and never get involved in a fight. Girls are simply more cunning. Their assaults are more devious. Males are settling a dispute, which is solvable. Females aren't. Their issue has to do with who gets what permanently. Females are just different from males in this way. If you want to be honest, there is no getting around it, and it has been what I've seen from the bench and hasn't changed much in all these years.

No doubt, Judge Rutter is not entirely wrong about some of the distinctions he makes with respect to girls; however, the challenges that girls face on the streets of their neighborhoods are also not as simple to avoid as he makes them out to be—like boys, girls in Melrose Park and Lee are also called on at some point to show their mettle. What in actuality distinguishes the situation for boys and girls most is the content over which they fight—money and drugs for boys and he-said, she-said situations for girls—and the related weapon use by boys. It is important to draw attention to the fact, though, that not every fight that a male youth in Melrose Park and Lee engages in is related to money or drugs. Boys are in no way immune to fighting over things that "don't really matter" when they are blinded by their rage.

Incidents that threaten the reputation of a boy are associated with a wide range of circumstances similar to how it is for girls; often it is the extremes that are the focus of interest and which come to define the collective sense of a situation. However, despite the particular style of expression or immediate content, the issue of respect for both males and females is a primary driving force where the resort to physical violence is concerned.

It is no surprise that judges in the Philadelphia juvenile justice system seem to be gradually changing their view about the violence potential of female youths as female cases have come to more routinely appear on their dockets. Almost every judge I spoke with indicated that he or she expected the presence of girls in their courtroom to increase, not decrease, over the coming years. Most also agreed that, if in fact this turns out to be the case and their discretion on the bench continues to be limited, girls would receive even stiffer penalties than they have known up to now.

Perhaps most important, the majority of judges who spoke with me did not feel that the judicial reform that swept the nation in response to the rising rate of youth violence beginning in the late 1980s supported the best interests of the child or, for that matter, the public. I would say that most perceived the Youth Violence Act of 1994,[11] which took away a great deal of discretion from the bench, as importantly diverging from the basic belief in a rehabilitative approach and separate treatment for juveniles and, over time, with changing the way juvenile justice was thought about and delivered in this country.

My discussions with judges left me with the distinct impression that, if it were up to them, greater discretion would be returned to the bench. Some judges were even in favor of removing status offenses—minor infractions that are only illegal for children—from the juvenile justice system altogether; these offenses (for example, shoplifting, running away, truancy, consuming alcohol) account for a large percentage of the charges that bring female youths into the court system. In addition to being in favor of prosecution and sentencing reform, criminal justice personnel at all levels were in favor of seeing new models of services developed specifically for girls. While such changes have been historically called for whenever a spike in the female youth arrest rate occurs, perhaps because the number of female youths processed by the juvenile system has grown so significantly this time, the call for more-specialized and better services will actually yield results. Indeed, in 2003, the U.S. Office of Juvenile Justice called for the compilation of a new generation of research on female delinquency to better understand its causes and trajectory. To this end, the National Girls Study Group was created by the Office of Juvenile Justice and Delinquency Prevention in 2004 (Zahn et al., 2008). While the increase in female delinquency research could in no way be seen as being prolific, the field shows important signs of growth and has put forth more sophisticated ways of conceptualizing why girls fight. Needless to say, it is extremely important for research in this area to be built on.

Law Enforcement

For police in Melrose Park and Lee, the strategy for keeping order is built around maintaining a greater sense of dominance. Residents in these areas often do not feel that the police presence in their community is meant to protect them. James Baldwin graphically described ghettos as "occupied territory" where police keep an eye on the inhabitants, making sure they stay in their place—in effect, playing the role of the colonial army "shifting cultural taboos" (*Nation*, 1966).To a degree, residents of Melrose Park and Lee express a similar conviction, though in their own terms. They see the police as coming around only to haul someone in after a problem has already broken out and not protecting the streets in the first place. They see policing as part and parcel of the wider system of structural inequalities that exerts control over their lives on a daily basis.

For the police, the incidence of violence is at best suppressed. Though their presence momentarily checks behavior, the unspoken understanding between police and residents—and often the spoken, as well—is that trouble will boil up again. Elijah Anderson argues that Black males have a clear sense of how they are perceived by the police (1999). This attitude leads to a script of suspicion that often can provoke the same violence it proposes to contain. Again, not much has been written to date about the attitudes that police have toward females where violence is concerned.

In my ride-alongs with police, I got to observe the exchange between residents of Lee and a handful of officers, though most of my ride-alongs were with one particular officer, Sergeant Palazzio. These ride-alongs also gave me the opportunity to witness altercations between females or domestic disputes between males and females. Just as residents sensed that the police disparagingly viewed them, the police, on a nightly basis, were made to understand the contempt that most residents felt toward them. Although Sergeant Palazzio and many of the officers that I got to know understood that the "system" went far to undermine the efforts of families and that many youths growing up in Lee "did not have a fair shot," it was clear that the disdain that the officers felt directed at them made it hard for them to sustain sympathy for the people with whom they came in contact. In large part, their sympathy was replaced by a bootstrap mentality that asserted that individuals needed to overcome their hardship and take responsibility for their lives. Police frequently viewed residents in Melrose Park and Lee as having taken the easy way out to pursue more immediate gratifications, referencing their own difficult backgrounds as evidence that one made their own luck. Girls who had brushes with police were seen in an even worse light, as they defied expectations not only with respect to personal responsibility but also with respect to gender. Like education and criminal justice personnel, the police I came in contact with typically viewed female youths as being much more difficult to manage than male youths. As Sergeant Palazzio reflected:

> You can rationalize more with a male. Females are more hot-headed. They want to talk. Have their say. Male officers will often call for a female officer to avoid having to arrest a girl. It's her foul mouth, or maybe she is going to say a male officer made a sexual move on her. It's also the case that sometimes a male officer will let a girl pass so he doesn't have to go through the hassle of waiting for a female officer, which can take a while. Like if it's at the end of his shift. It all depends. I've seen it all. There's a lot that goes on out here that most people don't know about, don't want to know about, and wouldn't believe if you told them about it.

Chief Harris brings up similar themes, as well as referring to how fights between females escalate:

> Females are sneakier. They use what they have at their disposal. The biggest street battles start with two women. They bring out all the

stops. Get their friends, their family—in the end it comes down to a lot of people. For males, it's not so much propriety over females. They go through different females. Females will try to disfigure other females. It's really hard to talk them down. It's not that you can't reason with females. You just have to talk to them in a way that makes them feel like you understand what's important to them. I guess that's the way it is with anybody. When you have officers who don't really know how to get to that level with a female, I think that's when you start to have a problem, and then you have a situation that's much more difficult to resolve.

Here again the theme of girls being "emotional" is quickly brought to the foreground. Girls' styles of provoking fights and keeping them going is indeed different from male styles and are experienced as more burdensome by officers. However, here again, it seems inaccurate to cast males as not operating from a base of emotion. Nor does it seem accurate to conclude that girls cannot be reasoned with. I found that those officers whose egos were less easily threatened could intervene far better when breaking up a fight in which a girl was involved. If an officer provocatively challenged a girl or treated her in a demeaning way, typically, the girl would not take a step back but would raise the stakes even higher. Perhaps this is what police officers and other professionals in the community refer to, at least in part, when they describe girls as far more intense than boys. As Kia explains:

> I'm not gonna let no fuckin' police officer treat me like a punk. I don't care if he locks me up. If I didn't do something, I ain't gonna shut my mouth 'cause someone tells me to. I'm gonna defend myself. Just because some police officer has a badge, that don't mean nothing to me. That doesn't make it right. I don't be needing to show respect if someone ain't respecting me. The police should be respecting people more.

One can especially hear in Kia's words the importance that she places on not being wrongly blamed for something that she did not do. Rather than losing her voice, as girls often do in school, as she puts it, she "defends" herself. When devaluation occurs directly and in a physical way, girls seem more able to counter it. In school where many feel inadequate, they more often withdraw. But Allie says:

If I did something wrong, I'm not gonna lie or make a fuss. It's just that I don't like to be told I did something when I didn't. And that happens a lot with police. They be coming at you like you're a criminal or something. They don't even check to see what really happened or nothing. Someone be minding their business, and then all of a sudden they [the police] just make a lot of assumptions, and that's why people get angry at them all the time. They just come and get in your face, and that ain't right.

Allie reiterates the theme of being wrongly blamed, though she suggests that she would be willing to take responsibility where indicated. However, it was my sense that most girls were hypersensitive to the police challenging them in part because of how they were approached but also because they generally experienced authority figures as humiliating them rather than helping them.

Indeed, I found that officers would frequently comment disparagingly among themselves about girls. Girls who fought were frequently referred to as "wild girls" and "bitches." Anthony, a lieutenant with over 20 years on the police force, described female fights as "bitch fights." The term was not uncommon among both male and female officers. Interestingly, while police perceived girls to be "more emotional" in their responses, they often characterized their actions as radically "unfeeling." Lieutenant Driscoll explains:

Young girls, their fighting is not usually self-defense. They're usually the aggressors. We usually get calls when there are dangerous weapons involved. Knives, bottles, box cutters, not often guns. Most of the crimes by females are directed toward other females. No regard for anyone else's welfare. More callous. Their tolerance level is short. You wouldn't think that girls could be so hard, but they can be. That was a new thing for me when I first came onto the force, and it has only gotten to be more shocking since. Girls can really be intense.

Lieutenant Driscoll characterizes girls as manifesting a lesser regard for others than boys typically do, a characterization I found to be not at all uncommon. Yet again, it is hard to reconcile how a male who shoots and possibly kills another male could be thought of as having any more regard for his victim or of not being callous, though the police typically cast female youths who engage in violence—and not boys—in that light.

One can speculate that the police start from the position that violence carried out by female youths is far more out of control, given that male violence is considered normative while female violence is not. Perhaps the violent girl seems more unfeeling and devious because she is expected to be self-sacrificing, whereas this is not the case for boys.

Lastly, it is well understood that the police do not apprehend combatants in most of the street fights in Melrose Park and Lee and that when a weapon is involved, or a large crowd gathers, the police are more likely to be called. On the occasions when I saw a large group of females fight one another, or I entered a household where a disturbance was reported among several females, I did in fact witness the readiness of female youths and often their female elders to "fight to the end" if they were not stopped. "Being heard" and "not being wronged" seemed to be of ultimate importance to females. Dynamically, the two together may help explain why the police perceive females to fight as intensely as they do.

While the typical narrative offered by professionals from a wide range of areas reduces to the message "girls are naturally difficult and more trouble to handle than boys," it requires moving beyond this initial characterization for a more dimensional and realistic picture to come into focus. For example, although when girls engage in fights they may indeed be hard to calm down, if they feel like their concerns are heard, they will show themselves to be quite capable of speaking frankly and rationally about situations. Indeed, once beyond the initial question of trust, professionals uniformly report that girls tend to form more open relationships with them than boys do. Thus, while gaining the trust of a girl may at first pose a serious challenge, for professionals who stay the course, there is a chance to genuinely connect with them. The distinction is especially significant in that it represents a window of opportunity for intervention.

7

Conclusion

The stories of girls who resort to violence in Melrose Park and Lee are new stories in the sense that the motivations behind girls' violent behavior have historically been obscured by the society within which they live—and, in large measure, by social science over the past 100 years. Other motivations more palatable to societies long uncomfortable with the phenomenon of females engaging in physical aggression have been substituted. In this book, which is based on hundreds of conversations with low-income girls, their friends, their families, the professionals in their neighborhoods, and a wide range of persons encountered along the way, I have sought to uncover how social, cultural, and individual factors work together to explain why girls in some low-income neighborhoods fight. Rather than simplifying the immense complexity of these girls' lives, I have purposely sought to maximize the number of extractable factors to be analyzed. Not surprisingly, I find that girls fight for reasons that are far more complex than the stereotypes and generalities that have typically been put forth to explain their aggressive behavior. I support intervention on the level of public policy and institutional reform, not just with the girls and their families who live in high crime areas and who engage in violence.

Historically, the consideration of violence through the lens of gender has almost exclusively focused on females as victims rather than as agents who engage in physical aggression. Throughout much of the 20th century, the social sciences did not contribute to a substantive exploration or mapping of the subject much beyond this. Females who inflicted physical harm were essentially relegated to the realm of sensationalized media coverage rather than being the subject of serious research. Little if any credible scholarship existed to guide treatment or policy decisions regarding delinquent female youths. A cursory glance at the literature will bear out that it has taken many decades for females who engage in violence to be viewed as a legitimate area of scientific inquiry worthy of government and foundation funding. Fortunately, today when social scientists listen to the stories of girls who engage in violence, they are typically more sensitive to theorizing their aggression, including the role that gender plays in its framing and expression.

Indeed, findings in the field have begun to inform programming decisions at various levels, including in family court and criminal justice systems across the nation. A growing body of research now documents the effectiveness of gender-responsive programming for girls, although the dollars spent for such programs lag far behind the numbers of girls entering into the system. Whereas the inadequacy of services for girls is at least finally recognized—a meaningful victory in itself—the problem and its root causes are still to be corrected. Yet even with its oversights, a bona fide field now exists where there once was none.

On an ironic and cautionary note, while asking what is unique about girls' violence that is not shared by the opposite sex has added great value to the inquiry into female youth violence, it has also sometimes allowed what sets the sexes apart to blind us to what is generic to both of them. The attempt to bring needed attention to the separate issues affecting girls, by its very nature, has sometimes lent itself to conceptualizing violent behavior by males and females differentially and mistakenly assigning it different causal explanations. The inadvertent consequence of this has been at times to imply that what motivates violent females and males is necessarily different and, by extension, to dichotomize the emotional states that respectively underlie their will to commit violence. Such framing risks the possibility of constructing female youth violence as a separate phenomenon with little if any commonality with male youth violence. It suggests that females and males are fundamentally driven by different imperatives.

Nothing that I have discovered in the course of my study, however, makes that case. On the contrary, the data on which this volume rests illustrate that there is great overlap in the factors that motivate female youths and male youths to engage in violence; in essence, violence needs to be looked at simultaneously as both a gendered and an ungendered story and, perhaps most fundamentally, a human one.

Youth violence in low-income neighborhoods, whether carried out by males or females, is in large part a reaction to a sense of actual and perceived threat, as well as a compensatory attempt to increase one's security, both concretely and psychologically. In this study, I found that, contrary to its usual antisocial framing, violence often served to provide a sense of mastery and self-esteem for youths in the absence of adequate prosocial opportunities, in addition to presenting an arena for bonding as well as simply for enjoyment's sake. Rather than drawing a binary framework to explain why males and females in low-income areas engage in physical violence, it is more accurate to say that, while differences distinguish, similarities abound. Ideally, such a perspective would act as an integrating device for the study of violence without erasing important distinctions. There is much to be gained by moving toward a more-dynamic conceptual framework that can at the same time accommodate both greater intravariation and intersimilarity of attitudes by the sexes toward aggression.

While it is no doubt true that the still-embryonic field of girls' violence, which has taken shape since the mid 1980s, has produced a vastly improved growing body of empirical research compared with the scholarship preceding it, it is critical to emphasize that many key issues remain largely unexamined. The twin issues of race and poverty, which significantly structure the life worlds of the field's main subjects, have not received nearly their due attention, causing the inquiry into female youth violence to be insufficiently contextualized. Certainly, culture, race, and poverty are frequently cited when referring to the variables that motivate female youths to violence. However, the existence of such references does not mean that they have led to a meaningful inquiry into how the three operate on the ground to inform girls' use of violence.

On the contrary, the symbolic and social structure of impoverished minority communities that is so importantly implicated in why girls fight has not been adequately unpacked in most studies of female youth violence. Observers have often failed to consider the real implications that race, ethnicity, and class have on inner-city girls' identities, their learning styles, their behavior, and how they are perceived by mainstream society. Notably absent are in-depth discussions that include how neighborhood effects such as poverty, crime, mother-headed households, chronic high unemployment rates, underfunded schools, and poor housing operate to shape the feelings and attitudes that girls develop about endorsing and engaging in physical aggression.

In part, this circumstance can be attributed to the fact that the vast majority of research on girls' violence has been quantitative in nature: thus, even when measures of race and poverty are incorporated into research designs, local meaning structures associated with female youth violence do not get captured. It is well accepted in the field that there is a dearth of qualitative research on the subject. There are relatively few multi- and mixed-method designs (quantitative and qualitative research within the same research project) that blend a coarse-grained and a fine-grained view together. Regrettably, the majority of ethnographies that have more than marginally commented on female juveniles carrying out violence are quite dated—and the more recent ones, which amount to a handful, can only cover so much territory.

Beyond the methodological oversights and incompleteness outlined above, another reason that race and class likely have not been adequately unpacked with respect to girls engaging in violence is partly due to the long-standing view of girls who aggress as being both socially deviant and morally deviant—that it is something either inherent about the girls themselves, how they were raised by their families, or the subculture that envelops their neighborhood, which accounts for their deviation from socially acceptable female norms—and hence, a deeper explanation need not be pursued. While for several decades now, poverty and race have been viewed as relevant to the study of male youth violence in inner cities, it is only recently that the highly sexist belief structure that has been a staple in explaining why girls commit violence has lost its legitimacy and framing power and no longer sets the stage of inquiry as it once did. The linkages that exist between neighborhood poverty and physical violence must be included as part of any analysis that hopes to reach a sophisticated understanding of the dynamics that underwrite girls' violence. One must consider how macro-level forces that produce social patterns and relationships that are structural in nature converge in the lives of female youths and their families and then, in turn, come to be expressed in the personal sphere. In essence, if we are to adequately investigate what it means for girls to commit physical aggression, we must take a less-narrow view of the subject and contextualize their aggression far more thoroughly than we have yet done.

When one does this contextualization, the instrumental function that violence has for girls in low-income neighborhoods also becomes much clearer. While one would not want to condone girls engaging in violence or minimize the harm that embracing violence can have for both aggressor and victim, it is similarly impossible to genuinely understand what motivates girls to use violence so frequently in their daily lives without recognizing the intrinsic value and benefits that violence can have for them. As discussed throughout this book, girls in high-crime neighborhoods that are characterized by higher rates of exposure to interpersonal violence commonly feel that they have no choice but to respond aggressively. Performing violence or threatening to do so is commonly seen by girls as a way to minimize their risk of physical threat, similar to the protective role that violence or its scepter has for male youths. When the instrumental function of violence for girls in high-crime neighborhoods is not credited, their violent behavior is simply viewed as being reflective of psychopathology and sheer gratuitousness. By definition, any girl characterized as "violent" could only be considered anomalous or "deviant" in some way, and not as behaving rationally. While in some cases this might be accurate, there are too many instances of girls' engaging in violence for this to be the default explanation for why girls aggress—for a girl to engage in a physical fight at some point was more the rule than the exception in Melrose Park and Lee. Lost is the fact that these girls are keen observers of verbal signals, body language, and the power relations of their environment.

Again, most of what has been written about violent girls has focused on their deficits and their risk factors for violent behavior, not the contextual underpinnings of their aggression.

Similarly, for boys, poverty and racial discrimination, as well as the devaluation communicated by mainstream society, result in an exaggerated emphasis on respect and increase the likelihood of confrontation for girls. Limited opportunities for mobility cash out as limited opportunities to acquire self-esteem, and a reputation for "handling oneself" works to offer youths a double benefit: it provides a measure of self-efficacy at the same time that it serves as a kind of "capital" in relation to other youths, the same way that money and social status do in middle-class neighborhoods. Without a doubt, the issue of fighting one's own battles and defending one's dignity and self-worth is central to the anatomy of girls' fighting. Despite the clear evidence for this, the trope of "respect" has not been afforded anything close to the same attention for girls as it has for boys. It sometimes is discussed in passing, but not developed in proportion to its significance as a justification and as a rallying point for entering into a fight.

What constitutes disrespect for girls in low-income neighborhoods, however, is not always the same as it is for boys; therefore, distinctions must be drawn along these lines. Girls generally tend toward perceiving disrespect in the form of personal slights and demonstrate a special sensitivity about their physical desirability to the opposite sex. Quite the opposite, both male and female youths report that male youths fight over things that are far more "serious" in nature—typically street drugs and money. For both sexes, one's sense of felt dignity is centrally at stake. It is the issues around which dignity norms are constructed that sometimes vary. From these norms, concrete rules of behavior flow, which are gender bound and contextually specific to shared neighborhood understandings. The role of humiliation, generally thought to be a precursor to male violence, should be equally a matter of concern when females are being studied.

Contrary to what is portrayed in the media and what many think, girls tend to fight more than boys do in inner-city neighborhoods because of the special dangers that surround boys fighting in those areas. Boys are far more apt to be involved in drug-related business than girls, and therefore they are far more likely to carry weapons. Consequently, they are actually less inclined to enter into a street fight over a small matter, given the increased chance that it might turn deadly. Conversely, girls are more likely to allow the he-said, she-said exchanges to escalate into physical altercation. Both male and female youths report this to be the case in Melrose Park and Lee. Rather than being anomalous, my research suggests that the actual incidence of street fighting by female adolescents in impoverished urban neighborhoods has been significantly underestimated in official statistics. This underreporting must be considered if one is to get a true picture of the phenomenon and what needs to be done to address it.

This said, common sense also suggests that, since not every boy engages in drug selling or carries a weapon, the linking of male violence to serious violence is not as neatly correlated as many assume it to be. Such binary characterizations of the relationship that the different sexes have toward violence are far too superficial. As with girls, we know relatively little about everyday fighting by males that does not result in serious injury or arrest, or how depression and other psychological factors influence a boy's resort to physical aggression. Again, what we do know is that both genders go to great lengths to avoid being labeled a "punk" because the label almost certainly guarantees further victimization—and as such, both males and females have to retaliate in some form or fashion to stave off being viewed as an easy mark or "enemy." It would be accurate to say that, for adolescents, violence as a prevention strategy cuts across genders. It is a strategy that is adopted by both younger and older adolescents, though sometimes in different ways and to different degrees, depending on a host of factors, of which gender is significant, though it is certainly not the only element.

The question is how to factor in gender without explaining too much or too little by it. While the needs and desires that drive male and female aggression often have shared origins (stressful community-based conditions like poverty and high unemployment set the stage for violence and confrontation to ensue), the gendered organization of these shared origins (how they are internalized and expressed) is closely linked to the range of behavior options that a particular community sanctions with regard to each of the sexes. At bottom, what in reality determines whether violent behavior becomes a community level issue for males or females seems to be highly related to how ready one's immediate surroundings are to support its expression. When prohibitions against females engaging in violence are relaxed, this rather limited study suggests that its incidence is apt to increase. The immediate environment of Melrose Park and Lee are two places where relaxation of such prohibitions exists.

Moreover, to truly understand the dynamics of girls' violence patterns in inner cities, the lack of an incentive that girls in inner-city neighborhoods have to stay out of trouble must also be considered. The lack of mobility and prosocial structures open to youths in inner cities, especially those youths who do not excel in school, create a vacuum of opportunity. The usual inducements to stay out of trouble—a good job and the realistic possibility of a secure future—are out of reach for many of the youths in such neighborhoods. For those youths who see themselves as "going nowhere" and unlikely to escape the problems of persistent poverty, staying on the straight and narrow has far less real consequence and, often, appeal.

While girls frequently speak of promising career prospects and aspirations, it does not take much probing to see that, for many, their visions are built on little more than blind faith. While some girls espouse high-achievement narratives, despite having little material reason to believe they can realize their stated dreams, many other girls seem to not be bothered by the idea of starting adulthood with a juvenile or even an adult record. Rightly or wrongly, many female youths do not view having a record as meaningfully changing their life chances, or at least they verbalize this. With the nationwide sharp downsizing of the manufacturing sector over the past several decades, there are relatively few career paths out of poverty for young minority youths. Changing the attitudes of vulnerable youths in inner cities requires genuinely improving their prospects.

Unlike middle-class girls, inner-city girls grow up seeing the necessity of fighting. In neighborhoods like Melrose Park and Lee, physical aggression becomes an acceptable and normative response for girls. Street fighting is something that girls are expected to show themselves to be good at—there is no shame in fighting if you are a girl in Melrose Park and Lee; in fact, quite the opposite. However, by mainstream standards, whereas fighting has been considered "healthy" for growing boys, both within and outside of inner cities, this has never been the case for girls—indeed, physical aggression has been commonly referred to as a significant harbinger of crime and maladjustment for girls. This, of course, is not what the residents of inner cities like Melrose Park and Lee know to be necessarily true.

Reworking the Term "Violent Girls"

As underscored across many examples in this volume, girls choose among cultural understandings and practices based on a range of factors, and therefore one cannot simply anticipate how they will behave because of their demographic or geographic profiles. No doubt there are some generic trends we observe, however: "female youth violence" is not a single phenomenon, even though it is often talked about as if it is. It cannot be merged into one stick figure that represents all violent girls— even within the same social setting. While the stories of girls fighting in inner-city neighborhoods have a profound resemblance, unfortunately, the term "violent girl" suggests too homogeneous a phenomenon. The term, like many terms, functions to reduce symbolic and real complexity and, in so doing, is problematic.

Historically, the common assumptions that underlie the term "violent girls" have always been associated with white, middle-class communities. In such communities, females have been normatively conceptualized either as victims or, more recently, as perpetrators of relational violence. Mainstream society has offered no way to conceptualize physically violent girls without devaluing them.

Consequently, when the term "violent girls" is applied to girls in inner cities, it imposes a set of assumptions about proper behavior and roles that do not correspond to the lives or social realities of girls like the ones

I followed. The term does not convey that gender socialization in Melrose Park and Lee emphasizes the importance of a girl being able to defend herself. Rather, the discourse about girls' violence, especially in the media and via the lens of mainstream standards, centers on girls being out of control and dangerous.

Another way that the term "violent girls" has erroneously conveyed a homogenous phenomenon is by failing to distinguish between less-serious and more-serious acts of physical aggression. The everyday street fighting by girls that does not result in arrest typically falls below the radar of observation and is overshadowed by more-serious, though far less common, gratuitous attacks or homicide. The portrayal of violence by girls in gangs receives attention disproportionate to its numbers. For it is the non-gang-related behavior that is far more prevalent. In essence, the term sensationalizes the resort to violence by girls by focusing on the worst cases at the same time that it significantly underplays the commonplaceness of less-serious ones. In this way, what it really means for a girl to use violence in an inner-city neighborhood is lost. Sensationalism wins out over substance much of the time. The term "violent girls" in the most basic sense is a misnomer, in that girls who engage in physical aggression are "violent" only a small percentage of the time. In sum, to be classified as such is a rhetorical device, not a meaningful concept.

As argued throughout this book, to achieve a more-dimensional portrayal of why girls fight, distinctions and differences among girls must be preserved rather than paved over. Instead of trying to rehabilitate the term "violent girl," it would probably be best to limit its scholarly usage in the field, as, in reality, there is a range of scenarios in which girls use aggression. At the very least, attempts should be made to "situate" the term whenever employing it in its context.

The Double-Generation Dynamic

Too little has been said about the role that mothers play in socializing their daughters to engage in physical aggression. While this likely is due to a lack of awareness surrounding the dynamic, it also may be the result of scholars not wanting to appear that they are blaming mothers for their daughters' aggression. It is understandable that scholars would not want to provide ammunition for a punitive backlash against mothers, as there is a long tradition of mothers being blamed for their children's problematic behavior, both in and outside of the social sciences. Yet, if female youth violence in inner cities is approached in a contextualized manner, it is clear that why girls fight is firmly rooted in their harsh surroundings and not simply their mother's errant ways.

In this book, I argue for the close consideration of the role that mothers in inner cities play in their daughters' use of violence and means to do so without faulting mothers in the process. I problematize the stance that mothers and grandmothers typically take toward fighting in terms of the socioeconomic disadvantage of their neighborhoods and the structure of social relations that are strongly shaped by it. It takes a long view to see the whole picture as it is created and re-created. Mothers—and grandmothers—in inner-city neighborhoods like Melrose Park and Lee raise their daughters to adequately manage everyday situations based on their own experiences growing up and then those associated with being the head of a household in a crime-ridden neighborhood.

Mothers are realistically aware that, in such a setting, to be viewed as a force in one's own right is a plus. And, thus, mothers actively encourage their daughters from a young age not to withdraw when challenged to fight. Even mothers with a history of antisocial or other troubling personal circumstances are not just simply passing down their problems to their daughters. Generally speaking, mothers see that the best way to protect their daughters from the harsh realities of the street is by instilling in their daughters both the importance of protecting themselves and the know-how to do so. The messages that a mother gives to a daughter about how to comport herself, and about her future, are surely not limited to fighting, although it could be misconstrued that way. One important message that many mothers convey to their daughters is that physical aggression has its place.

As mothers bring personal differences to the table and approach this educational task in more than one way, it becomes critical to investigate what contributes to the variability among them. Mothers, indeed, differ on a range of factors, including the degree to which they instruct their daughters to take the offensive versus fighting only when challenged to defend oneself. This study provides a preliminary understanding of what informs the variation among mothers and the implications that such differences have for their daughters, though it represents only a small step in this direction. Research aimed at further realizing the important role that mothers play in their daughters' relationship to aggression would expand our sense of the assumptions that girls operate on when they engage in physical aggression.

For the most part, the mothers in Melrose Park and Lee have grown up in a world not so different from their daughters, except for the fact that the streets today are even more dangerous than they once were. Most of the mothers fought when they were younger, and many continue to, or would, do so if it came down to protecting their family. As laid out earlier in this book, a girl relies on her mother, along with her relatives and female peers, to come to her aid if she is outnumbered or a fight becomes "unfair." While a girl's support network can be fluid, mothers are expected to maintain a steadfast commitment to defending their daughters. Certainly not every threat ends in a mother rolling up her sleeves to fight. Mothers use a wide range of strategies to ensure their daughters' safety and move them toward independence. Similar to the variation among girls in their propensity toward fighting, there is a variation among mothers. The important role that mothers play on many levels with regard to girls' fighting represents fertile ground not only for exploration but also for meaningful intervention.

It is noteworthy that this double-generational dynamic, whereby mother and daughter fight alongside one another, is an integral part of the anatomy of girls' fighting with no parallel among boys and their fathers or girls and their fathers. Although fathers tend to approve of their daughters' engaging in violence if necessary, they play a far smaller role in the process. This said, it would be valuable to inquire more carefully into the role that fathers play, as, no doubt, in many cases, their contribution is an important factor in how girls come to view aggression.

It is important to underscore that some female youths gravitate toward physical aggression because they themselves have been physically or sexually abused by one or both of their parents. However, neighborhood-level considerations play a significant role in the relationship that youths in crime-ridden areas have to physical violence. It is the social and cultural shared life circumstances that must be taken into account for all girls— both those who have and those who have not been abused—to help us understand why violence is so prevalent in certain neighborhoods. It is to this contextual backdrop of violence that mothers direct their concern and also their interventions.

The Institutional Response to Girls' Violent Behavior

Girls in Melrose Park and Lee perceive most of the authorities in their lives—their teachers, potential neighborhood employers, and the police—as viewing them as having little personal value. They typically see themselves as having limited horizons in school and in the work world and therefore invest their energies accordingly. They all too easily go from feeling inadequate to giving up. Once girls get to the point where they have fallen behind in school in a cultural context where learning is devalued, the odds are against them getting the help that they need. Since many girls feel that they learn "nothing" in school, they have little incentive to limit their aggressive behavior in school other than so they do not get sent to placement. Girls frequently attend school only so they do not get into further trouble with family or the juvenile justice system.

Without changes on a systemic level in education, there is less reason for girls in places like Melrose Park and Lee to feel like they have a future worth protecting. As an institution, education is in the greatest position to address societal ills, especially when children are afforded a rich learning environment from a young age. Readily available statistics, however, show the United States to be guilty of inequality in the economics of school districts and, in essence, offering "different" public educations to different citizens. While in the 1990s, most states adopted some form of outcome-based education, so-called increased standards did not meaningfully improve the quality of education for children in the nation's poorest neighborhoods. Girls encountered in the course of this study who, despite the inadequacy of their learning environments, showed the most educational promise, typically fought less.

Personnel in a range of neighborhood institutions in Melrose Park and Lee perceive girls who fight as being both more difficult to manage and as having more presenting problems than their male counterparts. This is the case, even though male youths often inflict more harm, fight with weapons more readily, and become involved with selling drugs. Indeed, despite all this, police and criminal justice personnel more readily identify mental health issues as driving girls' violence. In part, this is due to the fact that boys' psychological issues such as depression and anxiety are poorly understood. Male youth violence, despite its often antisocial character, is more apt to be framed in terms of instrumental reasoning. While girls are viewed as fighting over less, they are seen as doing so more vociferously and often more viciously.

The police are far less prepared to deal with female youth violence on a number of levels. With far fewer female officers on the force, the apprehending, searching, and transport of female youths presents a manpower challenge, as in many cases male officers must call for a female officer for assistance. The non-gang-related teaming up of females to fight—sometimes as many as 30 in one altercation—represents another management problem for police. The additional difficulty often translates into a felt sense of annoyance toward girls.

Broadly speaking, male and female police have more similar perceptions about girls' fighting than not. Both commonly speak more derogatorily about female youths who fight than about male youths who do so. Chauvinistic assumptions about girls and aggression are not just limited to male officers. Within police culture, the violent girl is simultaneously derided for violating gender norms—being hyperaggressive—and regarded as not being a true violent actor in her own right. She is both not taken seriously by the police and constructed as a "handful" all at once. Police typically have less understanding of the dynamics that influence girls fighting compared with boys. The subjective experiences and attitudes of police officers with regard to girls who aggress should be closely studied. The intersection of policing and gender has important practice and policy implications.

This differential perception of male and female youths has a paradoxical expression on the bench and in other levels of the criminal justice system, as well. Although in the courtroom female juvenile crime is typically not perceived to be as serious as male juvenile crime—rather more of a nuisance—at the same time, female youths tend to be perceived as more psychologically unstable than their male counterparts. Given society's greater willingness to incarcerate females these days, however, it is likely that the presence of female youths in all areas of the correctional system will continue to grow. As it does, changes in perception of female juvenile crime will no doubt follow, and they already have.

Right now, judges in the juvenile system have too few options to offer girls who are processed through their courts. To start with, they have far less opportunity to exercise discretion in sentencing matters than they once did. Within the confines of bad law, it is hard for judges to make good decisions. They are frequently left frustrated by the very decisions that they must make under the law. Indeed, in important measure, juvenile courts have taken on the character of the adult court system, gravitating more toward punishment than rehabilitation and providing less support to children and their families. The family court and juvenile justice systems across the country are in desperate need of far-reaching reform. The alarmingly high recidivism rate among juvenile offenders tells us that we are failing our youths and ultimately our nation on a most fundamental level.

The limited power of judges to divert youths, in particular, has hurt female youths, since girls often commit less-serious offenses than their male counterparts. Permitting judges more discretion and allowing them greater license to step out of the role of neutral arbiter could go a long way toward improving the disposition of female juvenile cases. As things stand, lack of judicial discretion inhibits the coordination of services that a girl receives.

Judges are also hamstrung by the lack of adequate treatment programs to which they can refer a girl once she enters the system. Programming for girls in custody has lagged way behind their increased entry into the system. Evidence-based practice approaches that guide the provision of assessment and treatment interventions are particularly in short supply. The most restrictive facilities are typically least equipped to provide treatment services. The good news is that, these days, the need for gender-specific programming and research is a recognized part of the juvenile justice conversation. Fortunately, equity in developing programs and facilities for male and female youths has become a more accepted value in juvenile justice circles. The bad news is that it will likely take years before girls' programming becomes a truly integrated part of the correctional system. The world of juvenile detention has historically been the province of male youths and, for all intents and purposes, still is.

As a rule, girls who are remanded to the juvenile justice or criminal justice system face multiple risks with regard to safety. The possibility of a girl being victimized sexually while in custody cannot be ignored. Stories of such exploitation are all too common. Level of care for pregnant adolescents confined to the juvenile justice system is also uneven among facilities. Teen mothers in the juvenile justice system do not uniformly have access to parenting education. Prenatal care for juveniles in detention is typically substandard. Administrative personnel in the juvenile justice system should develop best practices and recommendations for working with all girls in their care. Juvenile justice facilities should be held to health and mental health guidelines for female adolescents from the Center for Disease Control and Prevention. The promise of safety and ethical care must become an integral assumption for all youths in the custody of the state; otherwise, our right to remove children from their families and their homes is deeply subject to question, no matter the offense.

Sensitization of detention and correction personnel who are charged with supervising female youths must be factored into the equation when thinking about raising the standard of care that girls receive once they are placed out of the home. Even well-designed gender-specific programs require trained personnel for these programs to be administered successfully. Doing so would go a long way to improve facility practices. While detention centers may meet minimal operational standards, this unfortunately does not necessarily equate to their satisfactorily addressing the needs of their charges.

Moreover, when girls leave the system, there are also too-few transitional programs to help them return to their communities. Needless to say, transitional services are necessary if residential placement is to be anything more than temporary custodial care. Discharge planning and referral services are central to the success that female youths will have afterward. Residential or institutional care can only be of use to girls if it can help them feel valued and learn mutual respect. The number of female juveniles on probation has risen substantially since the early 1980s, but again, the access to gender-specific services that they need to help them turn their lives around and stay out of trouble is typically insufficient. While no doubt there are examples that do not fit the generalization, the signs are troubling.

There is a strong case to be made that, except for the most violent girls, in the context of the deficits and flaws of the current system, referral to community-based programs, including social service agencies and attendance centers, seems a better choice for helping girls. High rates of recidivism for girls placed out of the home are a robust indicator that we are doing something woefully wrong. Lastly, much work needs to be done on the policy level, as well as with regard to shaping cultural, social, and personal attitudes toward girls who aggress. How gender plays a role in discretionary decisions, charging practices, and sentencing recommendations—also the intersection of race influencing those decisions—are areas of immense importance, not only for the specific girls who enter the system but also for society as a whole. An overview of the juvenile justice system, policies, and decision-making as it operates with regard to girls should be a public health priority.

Advancing the Understanding of Female Urban Violence through Interdisciplinary Study

To deepen our understanding of what it means when girls fight, the field would be greatly served by studies that incorporate a dual level of observation into their analysis: that is, attend to collective themes, as well as address the variation that exists among individuals within the same setting. While low-income girls who engage in violence have received considerably more attention and research funding than ever before, especially girls who come into contact with the juvenile or criminal court system, the literature, to date, falls short in capturing how the intrinsic day-to-day reality of girls' lives shapes their relationship to violence and street fighting. Traditional methodology importantly limits the inquiry into female youth violence. The field would significantly benefit from thinking outside the box of traditional research methodology that cannot capture the dynamic reality of social behavior as it manifests on the ground. Descriptive ethnographic studies that investigate different aspects of how female youths in low-income neighborhoods think about and live violence is one such approach that is invaluable to advancing our present knowledge to this end. Unfortunately, only a handful of studies with a primary focus on female youth violence have been undertaken in this genre. By calling for the inclusion of both individual and collective factors into an analysis, one, in essence, is calling for a social science that is socially relevant and interdisciplinary in nature.

Most research methods, including ethnography, however, privilege either shared experiences and sensibilities or individual ones when explaining social phenomena. As such, data end up being overlooked or suppressed; both kinds of knowledge are necessary as individuals never act free of an environment, and it is only through people that environmental influences receive expression. Family and individual-level factors that introduce separate concerns and motivations—different life histories and experiences—further alter behavior. That social and cultural forces in Melrose Park and Lee help to produce and inform the proclivity of girls to fight does not explain why girls express that tendency differentially or the ways in which variations in this arena coexist. How as a field we address the variation among female youths who engage in violence and yet move toward consensus about definitions will determine the sophistication of our analysis and, ultimately, the conclusions that we draw.

None of the social sciences can fulfill their potential to offer sensitive accounts of human experience without giving both social processes and individual subjectivity their due. Consciousness and behavior are structured through interaction in a social world, in effect linking the processes of the individual psyche and the forces of the social field. Reflection on the self cannot be seen as an alternative to addressing society or social relations, nor can the privileging of collective representation offer sufficient insight into the individual. Both levels of analysis are mutually implicated in what it means to be human and what it means to engage in the social world. It is precisely within this analytic tension that the most exciting sites for social science lie.

To create these fertile spaces and bridge the divide between these levels of analysis, we need a dynamic concept of the interaction between the social world and psychological development and functioning—those psychic structures, conscious and unconscious mental processes, and personality traits that interact to maintain psychic equilibrium. To systematically consider a person in context requires that we contextualize their internal world, placing it on the cultural landscape and within the institutional framework that shapes it. Yet, unpacking the dense meaning inherent in a psychological and cultural story requires a critical departure from traditional research methodology, which splits the inner world from the outer world, takes the subject out of relationship with the observer, and, often, eliminates the relational and sociocultural contexts. It requires developing new methodology and new theories that conceptualize how individual psychology is shaped by culture and social structure, and it rests on a realization that the disciplines must work together.

Through presenting the views and experiences of several girls in their own words, I attempt in this book to show that girls' street fighting is the product of a confluence of sociocultural and more-individualized factors that are both tied to and go beyond the immediate performance of fighting (i.e., enhancing security, strengthening peer ties, looking at the degree of personal aggressiveness, and considering the extent of family problems). I attempt to show how the interplay of social and cultural forces with individual factors results in the production of violent behavior and events. I try to underscore that the study of girls' violence cannot be neatly fit into one academic discipline. Rather than minimize the fact that girls are both capable and willing to inflict pain in the course of a physical altercation, as a society, we must be willing to put aside our time-worn beliefs about violence being the province of males and commit to also understanding the role that fighting plays for girls in inner cities and elsewhere.

In sum, like every age, ours has its own unique needs that will inform what the study of human nature becomes. Like scholars before us, we are pressed to decide what we want our social science to be, whom it should serve, and to what ends. Considerations that influence this choice are deeply embedded in culture, as is the matter of who has the power to make those decisions and who has the power to carry them out. As social scientists as a group become more representative of the populations they study, one would expect the answers to these important questions to reflect a wider range of interests than in the past. Given our increasingly complex and rapidly changing sociocultural world, and the diversity of voices we as researchers and educators seek to accurately represent, conceptualizing the psychological state of individuals in relation to culture at the turn of the 21st century bears special relevance.

Notes

All names of persons and schools are pseudonyms.

NOTES TO CHAPTER 1

1. Anderson (1999) takes up the issue of respect in inner-city neighborhoods, with the main emphasis being on the meaning it has for males. In Anderson's analysis of the issue, the preoccupation with "being treated right" or receiving the deference that one is due is closely associated with racism, the humiliations of chronic poverty, and the sense of alienation that goes with them. See also Anderson (1990). The study reported in this volume is heavily informed by Anderson's work on males; I emphasize the similarities to his conclusions where girls are concerned, as well as draw out the distinctions when appropriate.

2. Historically, the term "violent girls" has been equated with sexually promiscuous and otherwise "deviant" girls. Early classic books and articles on the control of aggressive and sexually promiscuous girls, commonly cited together in this vein, are Lombroso and Ferraro, *The Female Offender* (1895); Freud, *Three Essays on Sexuality* (1905) and *Some Psychical Consequences of the Anatomical Distinction between the Sexes* (1925); and Pollak, *The Criminality of Women* (1950).

3. While Irwin and Chesney-Lind's 2008 article "Girls' Violence: Beyond Dangerous Masculinity" underscores the need to take context into account, in the end, girls' violence in this piece is primarily viewed through the lens of gender with the variables of race and class effectively fading into the background. Although the importance of gender as an organizing principle is not to be minimized, neither does it determine female actions or experience alone. Nonetheless, the argument advanced in the article—that the context surrounding girls' violence must receive greater attention—is a worthy one. As a second example, in Jody Miller's recent book *Getting Played: African American Girls, Urban Inequality, and Gendered Violence*, the author's "contextualized examination" (2008: 153) is basically an inquiry into "gendered power dynamics." Some exceptions where context is more systematically dealt with are Cobbina et al. (2008), Molnar et al. (2005), and Kroneman et al. (2004).

4. One such exception is Nikki Jones (2004). Jones's *Between Good and Ghetto* (2009), a more recent work, continues to explore the instrumental aspects of girls' using violence and the social world in which the girls live. Irwin and Chesney-Lind (2008) argue that researchers need to pay more attention to race in their analysis, but their focus remains on gender primarily.

5. Miller has written extensively on the subject of girls in gangs (e.g.,1998, 2001; Miller and Brunson, 2000). Although her work does not address the kind of street fighting that this book takes as its focus, many dynamics she writes about resemble the ones that the girls discussed here grapple with. As well, *Female Gangs in America*, edited by Chesney-Lind and Hagedorn (1999) is a useful volume on the topic of gangs.

6. Female youth homicide has historically accounted for a small fraction of murders. In 2005, females age 15–19 were nine times less likely to be involved in firearm-related deaths than male youths of the same age (Child Trends Data Bank, 2005). An example primarily of research on the topic of women who go on to kill is Morrissey (2003).

7. For instance, Maher (1997, 2004).

8. For example, Rajah (2006).

9. As might be expected given its disciplinary focus, sociology has done a better job of implicating context in a more-systematic way. For example, Wallace et al. (2008). From more of a public health perspective, see Yonas et al. (2007).

10. Anderson's work (1990, 1999) , which primarily looks at male youth violence, is built around this kind of an analysis. Jones's work (2004, 2009) follows in this vein where girls are concerned.

11. According to the Office of Juvenile Justice and Delinquency Prevention, in "a national survey conducted in the late 1980's, one of every thirty-six 10th-grade boys said they had carried a handgun to school in the past year. One in every one hundred boys brought that gun to school every day. In one U.S. city, one out of every fifteen 11th-grade boys had carried a handgun to school at some point" (OJJDP, 1997: ch. 2).

12. African American girls are three times as likely to be poor and three times as likely to be involved with the criminal justice system than white girls (OJJDP, 2000). This is no surprise, given that poverty and race afford substantially different material, social, and cultural resources with which to negotiate one's life, a scenario that translates into multiple risk factors, many of them associated with the increased incidence of violence

13. It is noteworthy as well that African American youth are typically overrepresented as perpetrators in the media while their victimization is typically underrepresented, especially in comparison with white victims (Dorfman and Schiraldi, 2001).

14. For a contemporary in-depth discussion of the characterization of the "bad girl," see Chesney-Lind and Irwin (2007). The book is unusual in the attention that it pays to the views of educators and criminal justice personnel.

15. Indeed, in the comparatively rare instances when the state placed girls in its custody over the first 75 years of the 20th century, it almost exclusively detained them in institutions charged with improving their moral character and not the penal-oriented reformatory schools to which most boys were sent to.

16. Valuable works on female arrest rate trends include Zahn et al. (2008), Steffensmeier and Haynie (2000), and Steffensmeier and Schwartz (2009).

17. Unless otherwise noted, data in this paragraph from Office of Juvenile Justice and Delinquency Prevention.

18. It is unclear whether the percentage increase of violent arrest rates reflected a true increase in offending or whether it was mainly if not entirely a function of changing arrest and sentencing practices.

19. Girls ages 12–19 currently make up roughly 25% of juvenile violent crime.

20. With reference to girls in gangs, Anne Campbell (1984) notes the importance of discerning how culture transmits representations of everyday theories of aggression to both males and females, of different ethnic groups and classes.

21. The experience of growing up black and female in America has been taken up more realistically outside of the social sciences in prose, poetry, and cultural criticism. In literature, see Toni Morrison, *The Bluest Eye* (1970); for a contemporary example in music, see Lauryn Hill's album *The Miseducation of Lauryn Hill* (1998). From a cultural criticism perspective, see *Killing Rage* by bell hooks (1996).

22. For an in-depth discussion of how the social organization of impoverished inner-city neighborhoods places a premium on respect, see Anderson (1999).

23. Artz (1998), L. Brown (2003), and Morash and Chesney-Lind (2009), among others, have put forth the gender-inequality perspective and suggest that girls fight against girls because they are safer targets than the males who in reality are the greatest threats to them. This perspective does not take into account the need for females to fight in order to protect themselves from the social vicissitudes of their neighborhoods.

24. Feshbach and Feshbach (1969) might be considered a precursor to more recent and more complex interest in this area in that they wrote about psychological aggression several decades earlier, though with regard to boys and not girls. The field as an established area of study, however, only came into its own since the late 1990s. For a recent consideration of the topic, see Underwood (2003).

25. This is not to say that quantitative research has no role to play in the field. Two examples of recent compilations offering valuable studies via this method are Putallaz and Bierman (2004) and Moretti et al. (2004).

26. There are few ethnographic studies on female youth violence. For two examples of book-length treatments of the subject, see Artz (1998) and Miller (2001). More recent ethnographic fieldwork on the subject, as mentioned earlier, is presented in Jones (2004, 2009).

27. Public discomfort with the idea of girls as offenders also limited the resources made available for programs and remediation.

28. In contradistinction, observations regarding the association between race, alienation, and violence have long existed in various literatures pertaining to males (Cloward and Ohlin, 1960; Valentine, 1968; Anderson, 1990, 1999; Bourgois, 1995; Devine, 1996; Gilligan, 1996). Nikki Jones's work (2004, 2009) is an exception with respect to its in-depth exploration of race, class, alienation, and girls' violence.

29. This was in keeping with both a natural science view of organisms being conjoined with their environment and with a line of thinking, beginning with Vico in 1725, that framed human nature as being historically and culturally determined (for background, see Vico, 1948 [1725]).

30. The basic epistemological challenge of the new science was to preserve the "dual existence of individuality and regular order, without collapsing one upon the other" (Heilbron et al., 1998: 119).

31. While Enlightenment science did not present a single unified vision of what the relationship among man, nature, and society was, or should be, the integrative approach characterizing the "new science" strongly influenced the kinds of questions being asked.

32. Sociocultural in considering how the surrounding social world shapes human experiences and perceptions, which is itself a human construction, and psychological in its focus on how individuals make and internalize meaning. Freud was first to approach this nexus armed with a psychological theory of mind—a framework within which to pursue a broader and deeper understanding of how experience is translated into meaning.

33. J. M. Baldwin's work stands as the first systematic use of developmental theory as a bridge between the study of social institutions and the study of individual function (e.g., Baldwin, 2001). He attempted to extend cognitive stage psychology to issues of social development and social organization. In this way, he anticipated other stage theorists such as Erikson (1950) and Vygotsky (1978), who attempted to systematically lay out the dual genesis—social and individual—of personality, cognition, and experience. Freud was first to offer an actual blueprint of how culture was psychologically internalized and then in turn regulated social life. Erikson was the first to systematically outline a stage theory of psychological development that viewed the entire human life cycle from the perspective of ego development in dynamic interplay with the culture's general aim and system.

34. Edward Sapir's work in this area spans from the early 1910s to the late 1930s. His work was unfortunately cut short by his early death in 1939.

35. Sapir viewed culture to be continually under construction in the course of human interactions and not a finished product (1932). While Sapir never lost sight of the fact that anthropology and psychology represented different analytical stances with respect to the same phenomena, he argued that bringing them together would lead to a more accurate rendering of the human condition. He specifically argued that anthropologists would have to get beyond superficial categories, such as kinship or ritual, to fully understand the symbolism implicit in patterns of culture (Mandelbaum, 1949: 201). The distinction was a major contribution at a time when both psychoanalysis and anthropology had constructed culture, though in different ways, as determinative of personality

36. Sapir thought this reciprocal influence was channeled through symbols associated with the history and environmental conditions of a particular group. Cultural systems resting on symbols served to socialize the group's members to generalized modes of conduct attributed to society, rather than to individuals.

37. His collaboration with Harry Stack Sullivan, as well as with other prominent psychoanalysts of the day—Clara Thompson, Karen Horney, and Eric Fromm—was a conscious attempt to formulate an interdisciplinary social science that would bridge the gap between social and psychological systems.

38. Again, regrettably, Sapir died before he was able to develop a systematic methodology to document his formulations, which left his ideas largely stuck in the realm of theory. Thus, while the overarching conceptual orientation of my study owes its primary debt to him, I look to other theories for help with narrative analysis or to address in some way the problem of moving from one realm of observation to another.

39. For a full description of the Listening Guide Method, see Camic et al. (2003: ch. 9).

NOTES TO CHAPTER 2

1. Of late, several neighborhoods in North Philadelphia, especially those closest to Center City, have undergone a measure of redevelopment and have seen the gentrification that usually accompanies such transition. I do not devote a great deal of space to this, as it has not been a major factor in Melrose Park and Lee.

2. The Delaware River, which separates the Commonwealth of Pennsylvania from the State of New Jersey, borders Philadelphia on the east, with the Schuylkill River winding its way through the city and eventually joining the Delaware River in the Delaware Bay.

3. "The downtown was bordered on the north and south sides by major railroad corridors that attracted dense concentrations of factories making locomotives, machine tools, scientific instruments, chemicals and pharmaceuticals, textiles and apparel, cigars, and dozens of other products. On the east and west, the downtown was bounded by two rivers, where shipping piers, lumberyards and coal depots, slaughterhouses, shipyards, and iron works likewise linked up with the region's web of railroads" (Vitiello, 2004).

4. Row houses were introduced into the country via Philadelphia. These structures abut each other and have shared walls. They are one of the most common residential structures in working-class Philadelphia.

5. Although railroad and factory workers of different racial and ethnic backgrounds often self-segregated in different working-class neighborhoods, it was not uncommon to find neighborhoods where different groups lived side by side, as well.

6. In chapter 5, I address the views of grandmothers and mothers in more detail.

7. On industry in Philadelphia, especially textiles, see "Philadelphia," in *Encyclopædia Britannica Online* (2009), at http://www.britannica.com/EBchecked/topic/455799/Philadelphia (accessed October 2, 2009).

8. In 1900, Philadelphia was the third largest U.S. city, with nearly 1.3 million residents; it grew to some 2.2 million by 1952, but then lost more than one-quarter of its residents and dropped to fifth place among U.S. cities by the end of the century (Vitiello, 2004).

9. Through the 1970s, the populations of Philadelphia lived primarily off industrial development and jobs (as well as the service sector jobs that supported industrialization). Mirroring broader economic trends, the city then shifted toward a more service-oriented economy in the late 20th century (Vitiello, 2004).

10. The book by William Julius Wilson captured the social transformation that was set in motion by rapid industrialization and driven by a free market that was inherently flawed and, in truth, very far from truly being free. The social milieu being talked about differed significantly from the environment that existed in inner cities in previous decades (W. Wilson, 1987: 58; Rose and McClain, 1990). In particular, the exodus of middle-income and upper-income black families from the inner city removed an important social buffer that could deflect the full impact of prolonged joblessness and industrial transformation (see also Hagedorn, 1988). Wilson's (1987:

56) thesis is based on the assumption that the basic institutions of an area (e.g., churches, schools, stores, recreational facilities) would remain viable if much of the base of their support came from more economically stable families in inner-city neighborhoods (i.e., those with vertical social class integration).

11. The increase in the arrest rate for female youth violence in Philadelphia mirrored national statistics. As indicated in the section on statistics in chapter 1, the dramatic nature of the increase was a reflection of the low base rates of female arrests for violence to start with, the shift to zero-tolerance policies for violence by police and in the criminal justice system, even where females were concerned, and the number of female youths engaging somewhat more frequently in violence. The higher arrest rates of female youth for violent interpersonal offenses took the criminal justice and correctional system by surprise.

12. Meda Chesney-Lind has written about the chronic underfunding nationwide of gender-responsive programs for girls in the juvenile system. Her emphasis has been on shedding light on the need for such programming and the misguided practice of funding beds rather than targeting intervention to the specific needs of the person who occupies the bed. In particular, see Chesney-Lind et al. (2002).

13. To read the judges' decision regarding decertification of White's case in 2000, see *Commonwealth of Pennsylvania v. Miriam White, Ruling of Judge Legrome Davis,* November 2, 2000.

14. West Philadelphia is comprised of 22 neighborhoods encompassing five zip codes.

15. Two of the African American girls who I followed most closely, Lakeesha and Tamika, go to school in Lee but live in West Philadelphia.

16. In order to spend time with girls at mainstream and alternative schools in Philadelphia, I sought general permission from the superintendent's office and then the principals at the particular schools. After revealing the purpose of my study, schools were suggested to me by personnel in the superintendent's office, as well as by personnel in the schools that I made contact with.

NOTES TO CHAPTER 3

1. Kruttschnitt and Giordano (2009) offer a comprehensive review of the literature of family impact on girls' offending, but it does not go too deeply into the normative aspect of families supporting girls' offending in inner cities because of neighborhood effects and other sociocultural factors. Tapper and Boulton (2000) address the issue of family support somewhat more thoroughly.

2. Leschied et al. (2001) emphasize what is wrong within the family as the driver for aggression. This study does not account for the cultural approval of girls fighting for the instrumental reasons noted earlier. Again, the research emphasizes the pathological and not the alternative cultural perception of violence.

3. See Margaret Zahn's discussion in *The Delinquent Girl* (2009) of the developmental literature on girls' violence with citations (i.e., Brooks-Gunn et al., 1997; Levanthal and Brooks-Gunn, 2000; and Obeidallah et al., 2004).

4. For a discussion of the importance of presenting a tough exterior as a strategy for protecting oneself, see Laidler and Hunt (2001).

5. With regard to violence as "capital" in inner cities, especially as it relates to males, see Anderson (1999).

6. While Anderson speaks mostly about males, his ideas also have much relevance for female youths, as well.

7. Apart from the different levels of physical danger that exist in inner cities as compared with middle-class neighborhoods and the different norms and values that largely control the expression of aggression by girls, many other distinctions between physical and social/relational aggression require further investigation. For instance, although Rachel Simmons suggests that social and relational aggression by girls reaches its peak between the ages of 10 and 14 (2002: 4), I found that the use of physical aggression by girls in Melrose Park and Lee was an important issue to be negotiated until age 16.

8. While it is certain that there are some girls who have never had a fight in Melrose Park and Lee or only one or two over their entire childhood, none of the girls I had contact with admitted to not ever fighting, nor were they or their mothers able or perhaps willing to direct me to a girl who had never fought. While I did not ask every girl or woman I came in contact with to introduce me to someone who never had a fight, a clear pattern of responses emerged and convinced me that fighting by females was indeed widespread.

9. Based on data from the District's Office of Transition and Alternative Education (*Notebook*, 2004).

10. Jones (2004) writes about the way girls will set each other off and the underlying reasons for this, and Morash and Chesney-Lind (2009) write about the "look," per se.

11. Female drug use, arrest, and incarceration rose in connection with the proliferation of drug networks and drug busts, though the majority of these arrests, like most drug-related arrests, were not for violent offenses (Maher and Daly, 1996). Also see Miller (2001), especially in relation to girls in gangs.

12. Miller and Mullins (2005), Ness (2004), and Laidler and Hunt (2001) are a few exceptions in their discussion of status.

NOTES TO CHAPTER 4

1. For a useful meta-analysis of the neighborhood effects literature, see Sampson (2002). For a more recent and excellent consideration of competing theories regarding neighborhood effects, see Sampson (2008). Together, these reports provide a valuable overview of the different kinds of questions often being posed by neighborhood-level theory and which need to be analytically separated out.

2. See also Zahn's recent discussion of the differential effects of neighborhood effects (2009), as well as Simons et al. (1996), Loeber and Stouthamer-Loeber (1998), Greenberg et al. (1999), and Howell (2003).

3. For a discussion of peer influences in inner cities associated with girls' using violence, see Giordano (2009).

4. The vulnerability to be rolled on is not limited to girls. Male youths use the tactic to intimidate and humiliate their male opponents, as well.

5. Little has been written about this, especially the role that mothers and other female family members play in a girl's security network.

6. There is a fairly extensive literature on self-esteem and aggression. For an overview on current debates in the area, see *Developmental Psychology* 41(1) (2005).

7. Bourgois (1995) talks about the cultural struggle for respect in the context of the drug trade, mostly as it pertains to males. For both males and females, the quest for respect is best thought of as a conglomeration of issues in relationship to a host of factors, including age, gender, and individual life history—not a single issue.

8. Burman (2004) writes about how girls defend their mothers against male violence but does not address girls' fighting for perceived slight against their mother's reputation on the street. This subject has not been taken up in any significant way in the literature.

9. Morash and Chesney-Lind (2009) comment about rage as it relates to girls resorting to violence.

10. As noted by Sunday et al. (2007), while physical abuse by mothers is less likely to lead to case documentation, its occurrence may be as frequent as with fathers. For an important discussion regarding the differential provocations leading to physical abuse associated with gender, see Obsuth et al. (2006), who find that physical abuse by mothers was not related to any form of aggression in adolescents but that exposure to physical abuse by fathers was linked to girls exhibiting aggression toward fathers.

11. One can quickly arrive at this conclusion by looking at the indexes of books on violence. For females, sexual abuse is characteristically listed with numerous references to sexual victimization, while references to physical abuse are rarely if ever present.

12. Whereas most of the literature on female child sexual abuse focuses on male predators, in recent years, more research on mother-daughter sexual abuse is being done. For a discussion of female-perpetrated sexual abuse, see Denov (2004) and Crawford (1997).

13. For a discussion about meanings related to Canadian girls fighting over boys, see Leschied and Cummings (2002).

14. Before the subject of girls' violence gained some credibility, girls' fighting was largely explained away as associated with "bad girls" or as "girls fighting over boys." Little appreciation was evident of the larger sociocultural structure that underwrites girls' violence or of the economic importance that a boyfriend has for a girl.

15. For a discussion of girls' weapon preferences, see Erickson et al. (2006). At least 25% of the girls interviewed in Philadelphia who reported previous violent attack said that they carried a knife. My own study suggests that girls loosely define what a "knife" is. Moreover, frequency of carrying the object ranges from once to always, with many scenarios in between.

NOTES TO CHAPTER 5

1. In the literature on female aggression, mothers are typically described as playing a role in socializing their daughters away from aggression, not toward it (e.g., Underwood, 2003). Here I actually suggest the opposite and underscore the normative aspect of mothers socializing for aggression.

2. Way (1996) reported the style of communication to be prevalent in their relationships with parents, their teachers, and their female friends, although typically not with boys.

3. See also Stevens (2005) and her book-length treatment of the subject, Stevens (2002).

4. Nancy Reagan's "Just Say No" campaign was a public service announcement campaign that was part of her husband's "War on Drugs" and was prevalent in the 1980s and 1990s. "Just Say No" was later expanded to the "War on Violence" and with regard to sexual abstention.

5. Over the past few years, it appears that there has been a resurgence of gangs in Philadelphia, although they still do not have the foothold they had in the city in the 1970s. The question has been raised whether the uptick in recent youth violence is gang-driven, although there is disagreement as to the answer.

NOTES TO CHAPTER 6

1. It is well accepted that schools in inner cities are notoriously underfunded compared with schools in more-affluent communities. Families who are doing better economically often send their children to private schools or move out of the area altogether.

2. Little has been written about the causes and management of female youth violence in inner-city schools, especially where girls are the primarily research focus. Where girls have been discussed, it has usually been in the context of studies that consider both males and females. Payne et al. (2009) is one exception.

3. One might productively consider the effect of being collectively devalued by the society that one lives in is an act of "symbolic violence." William Oliver (1994) has considered the internalized sense of oppression generated by mainstream culture as a major factor influencing black men to put each other down. No one has yet taken up the internalization of oppression in terms of females in any systematic way.

4. For more on the effect of teacher/student relationships on performance, see Muller (2001) and Knesting and Waldron (2006).

5. For a substantive analysis of urban education in the contexts of poverty and racial isolation, see Anyon (1997). For a historically contextualized understanding of poor outcomes from minority youths, see Neckerman (2007). For a gender-based analysis of specific reasons and timing of female youths disengaging from alternative schools, see Kelly (1993).

6. Shirley Ann Hill in *African American Children: Socialization and Development in Families* (1999) makes the argument that children in ghetto schools were better explained by characteristics of the educational system (i.e., poor teacher training and inadequate classroom resources) than by individual factors.

7. An early consideration is McCord et al. (2001), which offers a good overview of changing arrest patterns for girls. See also Chesney-Lind and Pasko (2003).

8. For a good analysis of the issue of transferring violent youthful offenders into the adult system in the state of Pennsylvania, see Myers (2003).

9. The penalties for so-called status offenses by girls has historically been harsher than the penalties that boys received for similar acts (e.g., Moyer, 1992).

10. The Texas Youth Commission (2007), *Review of Agency Treatment Effectiveness*, is one such study that supports the claim of reduced re-arrest rates of female youths who receive gender-appropriate and culturally competent services.

11. Among other things, judicial discretion was criticized on the basis of there being a great disparity in sentences for similar crimes. Some believed that judges and parole boards ruled too inconsistently when sentence determination was completely left in their hands.

References

Acland, Charles (1995) *Youth, Murder and Spectacle: The Cultural Politics of "Youth in Crisis."* Boulder, CO: Westview.

Adams, Carolyn; Bartelt, David; Elesh, David; Goldstein, Ira; Kleniewski, Nancy; & Yancey, William (1991) *Philadelphia: Neighborhoods, Division and Conflict in a Postindustrial City.* Philadelphia: Temple University Press.

Adler, Freda, & Simon, Rita (1979) *The Criminology of Deviant Women.* Boston: Houghton Mifflin.

American Correctional Association (1990) *The Female Offender: What Does the Future Hold?* Washington, DC: St. Mary's.

Anderson, Elijah (1990) *Streetwise: Race, Class, and Change in an Urban Community.* Chicago: University of Chicago Press.

———— (1999) *Code of the Street: Decency, Violence, and the Moral Life of the Inner City.* New York: Norton.

Anyon, Jean (1997) *Ghetto Schooling: A Political Economy of Urban Education Reform.* New York: Teacher's College.

Appleton, James; Christenson, Sandra; & Furlong, Michael (2008) Student engagement with school: Critical conceptual and methodological issues of the construct. *Psychology in the Schools* 45(5): 369–386.

Armistead, Lisa; Wierson, M.; & Frame, C. (1992) Psychopathology in incarcerated juvenile delinquents: Does it extend beyond externalizing problems? *Adolescence* 27(106): 309–314.

Artz, Sibylle (1998) *Sex, Power, and the Violent School Girl.* Toronto: Trifolium.

Ask MetaFilter (1999–2008) Resources on urban blight? At ask.metafilter.com.

Baldwin, J. M. (2001) *Selected Works of James Mark Baldwin: Developmental Psychology and Evolutionary Epistemology.* Ed. Robert H. Wozniak. Bristol, England: Thoemmes.

Baskin, Deborah R., & Sommers, Ira B. (1997) *Casualties of Community Disorder: Women's Careers in Violent Crime.* Boulder, CO: Westview.

Beck, Allen, & Mumola, Christopher (1999) *Prisoners in 1998.* Washington, DC: U.S. Department of Justice.

Belknap, Joanne (1996) *The Invisible Woman: Gender, Crime, and Justice.* Belmont, CA: Wadsworth.

Bewley, Joel, & Hefler, Jan (2006) Four killings put 2006 total over '05 top. *Philadelphia Inquirer,* December 11. At http://findarticles.com/p/articles/mi_kmtpi/is_200612/ai_n16975780 (accessed 8/29/07).

Bleyer, Jennifer (2000) USA: Touring the real Philly. At http://corpwatch.org/article. php?id=703 (accessed 8/12/07).

Block, Jeanne (1984) *Sex Role Identity and Ego Development.* San Francisco: Jossey-Bass.

Blos, Peter (1982) *The Adolescent Passage: Developmental Issues.* New York: International Universities Press.

Blumstein, Alfred, & Wallman, Joel, eds. (2000) *The Crime Drop in America.* Cambridge: Cambridge University Press.

Bourdieu, Pierre (1977) *Outline of a Theory of Practice.* Cambridge: Cambridge University Press.

Bourgois, Phillipe (1995) *In Search of Respect: Selling Crack in El Barrio.* Cambridge: Cambridge University Press.

Brooks-Gunn, J.; Duncan, G.; & Aber, J. L., eds. (1997) *Neighborhood Poverty I: Context and Consequences for Children.* New York: Russell Sage.

Brotherton, David (1996) Smartness, toughness, and autonomy. *Journal of Drug Issues* 26: 261–277.

Brown, Lyn Mikel (2003) *Girlfighting: Betrayal and Rejection among Girls.* New York: New York University Press.

Brown, Lyn, & Gilligan, Carol (1992) *Meeting at the Crossroads: Women's Psychology and Girls' Development.* Cambridge, MA: Harvard University Press.

Brown, W. K. (1977) Black female gangs in Philadelphia. *International Journal of Offender Therapy and Comparative Criminology* 21: 221–228.

Burman, Michelle (2004) Turbulent talk: Girls' making sense of violence. In *Girls' Violence?,* ed. C. Alder & A. Worral, pp. 81–104. Albany: SUNY Press.

Camic, Paul Marc; Rhodes, Jean; &Yardley, Lucy, eds. (2003) *Qualitative Research in Psychology: Expanding Perspectives in Methodology and Design.* Washington, DC: American Psychological Association.

Campbell, Anne (1984) *The Girls in the Gang: A Report from New York City.* Cambridge, UK: Blackwell.

—— (1987) Self-definition by rejection: The case of gang girls. *Social Problems* 34(5): 451–466.

—— (1993) *Out of Control: Men, Women, and Aggression.* London: Pandora.

Chesney-Lind, Meda (1989) Girls' crime and woman's place: Toward a feminist model of female delinquency. *Crime and Delinquency* 35(1): 5–29.

—— (1992) *Girls, Delinquency, and Juvenile Justice.* Pacific Grove, CA: Brooks.

—— (1997) *The Female Offender: Girls, Women, and Crime.* Thousand Oaks, CA: Sage.

Chesney-Lind, Meda; Arts, Sibylle; & Nicholson, Diana (2002) Girls' delinquency and violence: Making the case for gender-responsive programming. In *Handbook of Violence,* ed. Lisa A. Rapp-Paglicci, Albert R. Roberts, & John S. Wodarski, pp. 190–214. Hoboken, NJ: Wiley.

Chesney-Lind, Meda, & Hagedorn, John, eds. (1999) *Female Gangs in America.* Chicago: Lake View.

Chesney-Lind, Meda, & Irwin, Katherine (2007) *Beyond Bad Girls: Gender, Violence, and Hype.* New York: Routledge.

Chesney-Lind, Meda, & Pasko, Lisa, eds. (2003) *Girls, Women, and Crime: Selected Readings.* Thousand Oaks, CA: Sage.

Child Trends Data Bank (2005) Teen homicide, suicide, and firearm death. At http://www.childtrendsdatabank.org/indicators/70ViolentDeath.cfm (accessed 7/10/09).

Chilton, Ronald, & Datesman, Susan (1987) Gender, race and crime: An analysis of urban trends: 1960–1980. *Gender and Society* 1(2): 152–171.

ChrisV's Variety Blog (2007). The bodies fell, and the numbers rose. January 16. At http://chrisv82.blogspot.com/2007/01/bodies-fell-and-numbers-rose.html (accessed 7/8/07).

Cloward, Richard, & Ohlin, Lloyd (1960) *Delinquency and Opportunity: A Theory of Delinquent Gangs.* New York: Free Press.

Cobbina, Jennifer; Miller, Jody; & Brunson, Rod K. (2008) Gender, neighborhood risk, and risk avoidance strategies among urban African American youth. *Criminology* 46: 501–537.

Commonwealth of Pennsylvania v. Miriam White, Ruling of Judge Legrome Davis, November 2, 2000. At http://courts.phila.gov/pdf/opinions/whiteruling.pdf (accessed 9/8/08).

Crawford, Colin (1997) *Forbidden Femininity, Child Sexual Abuse, and Female Sexuality.* Burlington, VT: Ashgate.

Crick, Nicki; Ostrov, Jamie; Appleyard, Karen; Jansen, Elizabeth; & Casas, Juan (2004) Relational aggression in early childhood: "You can't come to my birthday party unless . . ." In *Aggression, Antisocial Behavior and Violence among Girls: A Developmental Perspective,* ed. Martha Putallaz & Karen L. Bierman, pp. 71–89. New York: Guilford.

Crick, Nicki; Werner, Nicole; Casas, Juan; Obrien, K.; Nelson, David; Grotpeter, Jennifer; & Marion, K. (1999) Childhood aggression and gender: A new look at an old problem. In *Nebraska Symposium on Motivation,* ed. D. Bernstein, pp. 75–141. Lincoln: University of Nebraska Press.

Daly, Kathleen, & Maher, Lisa (1998) *Criminology at the Crossroads: Feminist Readings in Crime and Justice.* New York: Oxford University Press.

Darnell, Regna (1990) *Edward Sapir: Linguist, Anthropologist, Humanist.* Berkeley: University of California Press.

Darnell, Regna, & Irvine, Judith, eds. (1994) *Collected Works of Edward Sapir.* Berlin: Mouton de Gruyter.

Denov, Myriam S. (2004) *Perspectives on Female Sex Offending: A Culture of Denial.* Burlington, VT: Ashgate.

Devine, John (1996) *Maximum Security: The Culture of Violence in Inner-City Schools.* Chicago: University of Chicago Press.

DiIulio, John (1995) The coming of the super-predators. *Weekly Standard,* November 27, 23–28.

——— (1996) Broken bottles: Alcohol, disorder, and crime. *Brookings Review* 14: 14–17.

Dollard, John (1939) *Frustration and Aggression.* New Haven, CT: Yale University Press.

Dorfman, Lori, & Schiraldi, Vincent (2001) *Off Balance: Youth, Race, and Crime in the News.* Building Blocks for Youth. Available at www.buildingblocksforyouth.org/media/.

Downs, Anthony (1997) The challenge of our declining big cities. *Housing Policy Debate* 8(2): 359–408.

Erickson, Patricia G.; Butters, Jennifer E.; Cousineau, Marie-Marthe; Harrison, Lana; and Korf, Dirk. (2006). Girls and weapons: An international study of the perpetration of violence. *Journal of Urban Health* 83(3): 788–801.

Erikson, Erik (1950) *Childhood and Society.* New York: Norton.

Feshbach, Norma (1969) Sex differences in children's modes of aggressive responses towards outsiders. *Merrill-Palmer Quarterly* 15: 249–258.

Feshbach, N. D., & Feshbach, N. (1969) The relationship between empathy and aggression in two age groups. *Developmental Psychology* 1: 102–107.

Figueria-McDonough, Josephina (1992) Community structure and female delinquency rates. *Youth and Society* 24: 3–30.

Freud, Sigmund (1905) *Three Essays on Sexuality.* In *The Standard Edition of the Complete Psychological Works of Sigmund Freud,* vol. 7, ed. James Strachey, pp. 135–243. London: Hogarth.

——— (1925) *Some Psychical Consequences of the Anatomical Distinctions between the Sexes.* In *The Standard Edition of the Complete Psychological Works of Sigmund Freud,* vol. 19, ed. James Strachey, pp. 243–258. London: Hogarth.

——— (1931) *Female Sexuality.* In *The Standard Edition of the Complete Psychological Works of Sigmund Freud,* vol. 21, ed. James Strachey, pp. 225–243. London: Hogarth.

——— (1933) *New Introductory Lectures on Psychoanalysis.* In *The Standard Edition of the Complete Psychological Works of Sigmund Freud,* vol. 22, ed. James Strachey, pp. 1–182. London: Hogarth.

Gilfus, Mary (1992) From victims to survivors to offenders: Women's routes of entry and immersion in street crime. *Women and Criminal Justice* 4: 63–89.

Gilligan, James (1996) *Violence: Reflections on a National Epidemic.* New York: Vintage.

Giordano, Peggy (2009) Peer influences on girls delinquency. In *The Delinquent Girl,* ed. Margaret A. Zahn, pp.127–138. Philadelphia: Temple University Press.

Greenberg, M. T.; Lengua, L. J.; Coie, J. D.; & Pinderhughes, E. E. (1999) Predicting developmental outcomes at school entry using a multiple risk model: Four American communities. *Developmental Psychology* 33: 403–417.

Hagedorn, John (1988) *People and Folks: Gangs, Crime and the Underclass in a Rust-Belt City.* Chicago: Lake View.

Hall, Judith (1978) Gender effects in decoding nonverbal cues. *Psychological Bulletin* 85: 845–857.

Hawkins, Darnell (1983). Black and white homicide differentials: Alternatives to an inadequate theory. *Criminal Justice and Behavior* 10: 407–440.

Heidensohn, Frances (1985) *Women and Crime.* New York: New York University Press.

Heilbron, Johan; Magnusson, Lars; & Wittrock, Bjorn, eds. (1998) *Conceptual Change in Context, 1750–1850.* New York: Kluwer Academic.

Henington, Carlen; Hughes, Jan; Cavell, Timothy; & Thompson, B. (1998) The role of relational aggression in identifying aggressive boys and girls. *Journal of School Psychology* 36: 457–477.

Hill, Lauryn (1998) *The Miseducation of Lauryn Hill.* Philadelphia: Ruffhouse Records.

Hill, Shirley Ann (1999) *African American Children: Socialization and Development in Families.* Thousand Oaks, CA: Sage.

hooks, bell (1996) *Killing Rage: Ending Racism.* New York: Holt.

Howell, J. C. (2003) *Preventing and Reducing Juvenile Delinquency: A Comprehensive Framework.* Thousand Oaks, CA: Sage.

Irwin, Katherine, & Chesney-Lind, Mesa (2008) Girls' violence: Beyond dangerous masculinity. *Sociology Compass* 2(3): 837–835. At http://socialsciences.people. hawaii.edu/publications_lib/BeyondDangerousMasc.pdf.

Jack, Dana (1999) *Behind the Mask: Destruction and Creativity in Women's Aggression.* Cambridge, MA: Harvard University Press.

Jacob, Joanna (2006) Male and female youth crime in Canadian communities: Assessing the applicability of social disorganization theory. *Canadian Journal of Criminology and Criminal Justice* 48(1): 31–60.

Jones, Nikki (2004) It's not where you live, it's how you live: How young women negotiate conflict and violence in the inner city. In *Being Here and Being There: Fieldwork Encounters and Ethnographic Discoveries,* ed. Elijah Anderson, Scott Brooks, Raymond Gunn, and Nikki Jones, pp. 49–62. Thousand Oaks, CA: Sage.

——— (2009) *Between Good and Ghetto: African American Girls and Inner City Violence.* New Brunswick, NJ: Rutgers University Press.

Kelly, Dierdre (1993) *Last Chance High: How Girls and Boys Drop In and Out of Alternative Schools.* New Haven, CT: Yale University Press.

Kling, Jeffrey; Ludwig, Jens; & Katz, Lawrence F. (2004) Neighborhood effects on crime for female and male youths: Evidence from a randomized housing voucher experiment. *Quarterly Journal of Economics* 1(January): 87–130.

Knesting, Kimberly, & Waldron, Nancy (2006) Willing to play the game: How at-risk students persist in school. *Psychology in the Schools* 43(5): 599–611.

Konopka, Gisela (1966) *The Adolescent Girl in Conflict.* Englewood, NJ: Prentice Hall.

——— (1976) *Young Girls: A Portrait of Adolescence.* Englewood, NJ: Prentice Hall.

Kroneman, L.; Loeber, R.; & Hipwell, A. E. (2004) Is neighborhood context differently related to externalizing problems and delinquency for girls compared with boys? *Clinical Child and Family Psychology Review* 7(2): 109–122.

Kruttschnitt, Candace, & Giordano, Peggy (2009) Family influences on girls' delinquency. In *The Delinquent Girl,* ed. Margaret A. Zahn, pp. 107–126. Philadelphia: Temple University Press.

Laidler, Karen, & Hunt, Geoffrey (2001) Accomplishing femininity among the girls in the gang. *British Journal of Criminology* 41: 656–678.

Lamb, Sharon (2001) *The Secret Lives of Girls: What Good Girls Really Do.* New York: Simon and Schuster.

Leadbeater, Bonnie, & Way, Niobe, eds. 1996. *Urban Girls: Resisting Stereotypes, Creating Identities.* New York: New York University Press.

Lederman, C., & Brown, E. (2000) Entangled in the shadows: Girls in the juvenile justice system. *Buffalo Law Review* 48: 909–925.

Leschied, A. W., & Cummings, A. L. (2002) Youth violence: An overview of predictors, counselling interventions, and future directions. *Canadian Journal of Counseling* 36: 252–264.

Leschied, A. W.; Cummings, A. L.; Van Brunschot, M.; Cunningham, A.; & Saunders, A. (2001) A review of the literature on aggression in adolescent girls: Implications for policy, prevention and treatment. *Canadian Psychology* 42: 200–215.

Levanthal, Tama, & Brooks-Gunn, Jeanne (2000) The neighborhoods they live in: The effects of neighborhood residence upon child and adolescent outcomes. *Psychological Bulletin* 126: 309–337.

Levins, Hoag (2002) Industrial history, sweet and sour. At http://historiccamden-county.com/ccnews37.shtml.

Loeber, R., & Stouthamer-Loeber, M. (1998) Juvenile aggression at home and at school. In *Violence in American Schools,* ed. D. S. Elliott, K. R. Williams, & B. Hamburg, pp. 94–126. Cambridge: Cambridge University Press.

Lombroso, Cesare, & Ferraro, William (1895) *The Female Offender.* London: Fisher Unwin.

Maccoby, Eleanor, & Jacklin, Carol (1974) *The Psychology of Sex Differences.* Stanford, CA: Stanford University Press.

Maher, Lisa (1997) *Sexed Work: Gender, Race and Resistance in a Brooklyn Drug Market.* Oxford: Oxford University Press.

——— (2004) A reserve army: Women and the drug market. In *The Criminal Justice System and Women: Offenders, Prisoners, Victims, and Workers,* ed. Barbara Raffel Price & Natalie Sokoloff, 3rd ed., pp. 127–146. Boston: McGraw-Hill.

Maher, Lisa, & Daly, Kathleen (1996) Women in the street-level drug economy: Continuity or change. *Criminology* 34(4): 465–491.

Mandelbaum, David, ed. (1949) *Selected Writings of Edward Sapir in Language, Culture, and Personality.* Berkeley: University of California Press.

Manke, B.; McGuire, S.; Reiss, D.; Hetherington, E. M.; & Plomin, R. (1995) Genetic contributions to adolescents' extrafamilial social interactions: Teachers, best friends, and peers. *Social Development* 4: 238–256.

McCord, Joan; Spatz Widom, Cathy; & Crowell, Nancy A. (2001) *Juvenile Crime, Juvenile Justice. Panel on Juvenile Crime: Prevention, Treatment, and Control.* Washington, DC: National Academy Press.

McKee, Guian (2004) Urban deindustrialization and local public policy: Industrial renewal in Philadelphia, 1953–1976. *Journal of Policy History* 16(1): 66–98.

Miller, Jody (1998) Gender and victimization risk among young women in gangs. *Journal of Research in Crime and Delinquency* 35(4): 429–453.

——— (2001) *One of the Guys: Girls, Gangs, and Gender.* New York: Oxford University Press.

——— (2008) *Getting Played: African American Girls, Urban Inequality, and Gendered Violence.* New York: New York University Press.

Miller, Jody, & Brunson, Rod K. (2000) Gender dynamics in youth gangs: A comparison of male and female accounts. *Justice Quarterly* 17(3): 801–830.

Miller, Jody, & Mullins, Christopher (2005) Stuck up, telling lies, and talking too much: The gendered context of young women's violence. In *Gender and Crime: Patterns in Victimization and Offending,* ed. Karen Heimer & Candace Kruttschnitt, 41–66. New York: New York University Press.

Molnar, B. E.; Browne, A.; Cerda, M.; & Buka, S. L. (2005) Violent behavior by girls reporting violent victimization. *Archives of Pediatric and Adolescent Medicine* 159: 731–739.

Morash, Merry, & Chesney-Lind, Meda (2009) The context of girls' violence: Peer groups, families, schools, and communities. In *The Delinquent Girl*, ed. Margaret A. Zahn, pp. 182–206. Philadelphia: Temple University Press.

Moretti, Marlene Marie; Odgers, Candice L.; & Jackson, Margaret A. (2004) *Girls and Aggression: Contributing Factors and Intervention Principles.* New York: Kluwer Academic/Plenum.

Morrison, Toni (1970) *The Bluest Eye.* New York: Random House.

Morrissey, Belinda (2003) *When Women Kill: Questions of Agency and Subjectivity.* New York: Routledge.

Moyer, Imogene L. (1992) *Changing Roles of Women in the Criminal Justice System: Offenders, Victims, and Professionals.* Prospect Heights, IL: Waveland.

Muller, Chandra (2001) The role of caring in the teacher-student relationship for at-risk students. *Sociological Inquiry* 71(2): 241–255.

Murray, Charles (1984) *Losing Ground: American Social Policy, 1950–1980.* New York: Basic Books.

Myers, David (2003) Adult crime, adult time, *Youth Violence and Juvenile Justice* 1(2): 173–197.

Nation (1966) A report from occupied territory. July 11.

Neckerman, Kathryn (2007) *Schools Betrayed: Roots of Failure in Inner-City Education.* Chicago: University of Chicago Press.

Ness, Cindy (2004) Why girls fight: Female youth violence in the inner city. *Annals of the American Academy of Political and Social Science* 595: 32–48.

Newman, Katherine (1999) *Falling from Grace: Downward Mobility in the Age of Affluence.* Berkeley: University of California Press.

——— (2006) *Chutes and Ladders: Navigating the Low-Wage Labor Market.* New York: Russell Sage.

——— (2007) *The Missing Class: Portraits of the Near Poor in America.* Boston: Beacon.

Notebook (2004) Alternative school enrollment grew by 1,000 in 15 months. February. At http://www.thenotebook.org/newsflash/2004/february/alternative.htm (accessed 9/10/08).

Obeidallah, Dawn; Brennan, Robert; Brooks-Gunn, Jeanne; & Earls, Felton (2004) Links between pubertal timing and neighborhood contexts: Implications for girls' violent behavior. *Journal of the American Academy of Child and Adolescent Psychiatry* 43(12): 1460–1468.

Obsuth, Ingrid; Moretti, M.; & Odgers, Candace (2006) Disentangling the effects of physical abuse and exposure to inter-parental violence on adolescents' aggression across context. At http://www.sfu.ca/adolescenthealth/posters/INGRID_SRA_IPV_vs_Phys_Abuse_2006.pdf (accessed 10/15/2008).

Office of Juvenile Justice and Delinquency Prevention (OJJDP) (1997) *Juvenile Justice Reform Initiatives in the United States 1994–1996.* U.S. Department of Justice, Office of Justice Programs. At http://ojjdp.ncjrs.org/pubs/reform/contents.html (accessed 7/20/07).

———— (2000) *Female Delinquency Cases, 1997*. Washington, DC: U.S. Department of Justice.

———— (2001) *Female Gangs: A Focus on Research*. U.S. Department of Justice, Office of Justice Programs. At http://www.ncjrs.gov/html/ojjdp/jjbul2001_3_3/contents. html.

———— (2002) *Trends in Juvenile Violent Offending: An Analysis of Victim Survey Data*. U.S. Department of Justice, Office of Justice Programs. At http://www.ncjrs.gov/ html/ojjdp/jjbul2002_10_1/contents.html (accessed 9/9/07).

Oliver, William (1994) *The Violent Social World of Black Men*. San Francisco: Jossey-Bass.

Payne, Allison Ann; Gottfredson, Denise C.; & Kruttschnitt, Candace (2009) Girls, schools, and delinquency. In *The Delinquent Girl*, ed. Margaret A. Zahn, pp. 146–163. Philadelphia: Temple University Press.

Pollak, Otto (1950) *The Criminality of Women*. Philadelphia: University of Pennsylvania Press.

Putallaz, M., & Bierman, K. L. (2004) *Aggression, Antisocial Behavior, and Violence among Girls*. New York: Guilford.

Rajah, V. (2006) Respecting boundaries: The symbolic and material concerns of drug-involved women employing violence against violent male partners. *British Journal of Criminology* 46(5): 837–858.

Rhodes, Jean, & Fischer, Karla (1993) Spanning the gender gap: Gender differences in delinquency among inner-city adolescents. *Adolescence* 28: 879–889.

Rose, Harold, & McClain, Paula (1990) *Race, Place and Risk: Black Homicide in Urban America*. Albany: SUNY Press.

Sampson, Robert J. (2002) Assessing neighborhood effects: Social processes and new directions in research. *Annual Review of Sociology* 28: 443–478.

———— (2003) The neighborhood context of well-being. *Perspectives in Biology and Medicine* 46(3): S53–S64.

———— (2008) Moving to inequality: Neighborhood effects and experiments meet social structure. *American Journal of Sociology* 114(1): 189–231.

Sampson, Robert; Raudenbush, Stephen; & Earls, Felton (1997) Neighborhoods and violent crime: A multilevel study of collective efficacy. *Science* 277: 918–924.

Sapir, Edward (1930) The cultural approach to the study of personality. Paper presented at Hanover Conference of 1930.

———— (1932) Letter to Alfred L. Kroeber, May 24, 1932. Archives of the University of California, Berkeley.

Shaw, Clifford (1930) *The Jack-Roller*. Chicago: University of Chicago Press.

Simmons, Rachel (2002) *Odd Girl Out: The Hidden Culture of Aggression in Girls*. New York: Harcourt.

Simons, R. L.; Johnson, C.; Beaman, J.; Conger, R. D.; & Whitbeck, L. B. (1996) Parents and peer group as mediators of the effect of community structure on adolescent problem behavior. *American Journal of Community Psychology* 24: 145–172.

Spencer, M. B.; Cross, W. E.; Harpalani, V; & Goss, T. N. (2001) Historical and developmental perspectives on Black academic achievement: Debunking the "acting White" myth and posing new directions for research. In *Surmounting All Odds: Education, Opportunity, and Society in the New Millennium*, ed. C. C. Yeakey. Greenwich, CT: Information Age.

Steffensmeier, Darrell, & Allan, Emilie (1996) Gender and crime: Toward a gendered theory of female offending. *Annual Review of Sociology* 22: 459–487.

Steffensmeier, Darrell, & Haynie, Dana (2000) The structural sources of urban female violence in the United States. *Homicide Studies* 4(2): 107–134.

Steffensmeier, Darrell, and Schwartz, Jennifer (2009) Trends in girls' delinquency and the gender gap: Statistical assessment of diverse sources. In *The Delinquent Girl*, ed. Margaret Zahn, pp. 50–83. Philadelphia: Temple University Press.

Stevens, Joyce (2002) *Smart and Sassy: The Strengths of Inner-City Black Girls*. New York: Oxford University Press.

——— (2005) Lessons learned from poor African American youth: Resilient strengths in coping with adverse environments. In *Handbook for Working with Children and Youth: Pathways to Resilience across Cultures and Contexts*, ed. Michael Ungar, 45–56. Thousand Oaks, CA: Sage.

Sunday, Suzanne; Labruna, Victor; Kaplan, Sandra; Pelcovitz, David; Newman, Jennifer; & Salzinger, Suzanne (2007) Physical abuse during adolescence: Gender differences in the adolescents' perceptions of family functioning and parenting. *Child Abuse and Neglect* 32(1): 5–18.

Talbot, Elizabeth (1997) Reflecting on antisocial girls and the study of their development: Researchers' views. *Exceptionality* 7: 267–272.

Tapper, K., & Boulton, M. J. (2000) Social representations of physical, verbal and indirect aggression: Age and sex differences. *Aggressive Behavior* 26: 542–545.

Testa, M.; Aston, N. M.; Krogh, M.; & Neckerman, K. M. (1989) Employment and marriage among inner-city fathers. *Annals of the American Academy of Social and Political Sciences* 501: 79–91.

Texas Youth Commission (2007) *Review of Agency Treatment Effectiveness*. At http://www.tyc.state.tx.us/research/TxmtEffect/05_forward.html (accessed 8/14/08).

Thrasher, Frederic (1927) *The Gang: A Study of 1,313 Gangs in Chicago*. Chicago: University of Chicago Press.

Underwood, Marion (2003) *Social Aggression among Girls*. New York: Guilford.

U.S. Census Bureau (2000) *Census of Housing and Population*. At http://www.census.gov/prod/cen2000/index.html.

Valentine, Charles (1968) *Culture and Poverty: Critique and Counter-Proposals*. Chicago: University of Chicago Press.

Vedder, Clyde, & Somerville, Dora (1973) *The Delinquent Girl*. Springfield, IL: Charles Thomas.

Vico, Giambattista (1948 [1725]) *The New Science: Principles of the New Science Concerning the Common Nature of Nations*. Trans. T. G. Bergib & M. H. Fisch. Ithaca, NY: Cornell University Press.

Vitiello, Dominic (2004) Urban America: What it was and what it is becoming. Working Paper #15. At http://www.sp2.upenn.edu/america2000/wp15all.pdf (accessed 6/14/07, 7/24/07, 7/29/07).

Vygotsky, L. S. (1978) *Mind in Society: Development of Higher Psychological Processes*. Cambridge, MA: Harvard University Press.

Wallace, Don; Hirschinger-Blank, Nancy; & Grisso, Jeane A. (2008) Female-female non-partner assault: A political-economic theory of street codes and female-gendered culture in the contemporary African-American inner city. *Critical Sociology* 34(2): 271–290.

West, Cornel (1993) *Race Matters.* Boston: Beacon.

Whiting, Beatrice B., & Edwards, Carolyn P. (1973) A cross-cultural analysis of sex differences in the behavior of children aged 3–11. *Journal of Social Psychology* 91: 171–188.

Whyte, William Foote (1943) *Street Corner Society: The Social Structure of an Italian Slum.* Chicago: University of Chicago Press.

Widom, Cathy (1989) Does violence beget violence? A critical examination of the literature. *Psychological Bulletin* 106(1): 3–28.

Wikipedia. History of Philadelphia. At http://en.wikipedia.org/wiki/History_of_philadelphia (accessed 7/24/07).

———— Philadelphia. At http://en.wikipedia.org/wiki/Philadelphia%2C_Pennsylvania#_note-38 (accessed 8/19/07).

———— Philadelphia Naval Shipyard. At http://en.wikipedia.org/wiki/Philadelphia_Naval_Shipyard.

Wilson, James (1975) *Thinking about Crime.* New York: Basic Books.

Wilson, James, & Herrnstein, Richard (1985) *Crime and Human Nature.* New York: Simon and Schuster.

Wilson, William J. (1987) *The Truly Disadvantaged: The Inner-City, the Underclass and Public Policy.* Chicago: University of Chicago Press.

Wiseman, Rosalind (2002) *Queen Bees and Wannabes: Helping Your Daughter Survive Cliques, Gossip, Boyfriends, and the Realities of Adolescence.* New York: Crown.

Wolfgang, Marvin, & Ferracuti, Franco (1967) *The Subculture of Violence: Towards an Integrated Theory in Criminology.* London: Tavistock.

Yonas, M. A.; Ocampo, P.; Burke, J. G.; & Gielen, A. C. (2007) Neighborhood-level factors and youth violence: Giving voice to the perceptions of prominent neighborhood individuals. *Health Education and Behavior* 34(4): 669–685.

Zahn, Margaret, ed. (2009) *The Delinquent Girl.* Philadelphia: Temple University Press.

Zahn, Margaret A.; Brumbaugh, Susan; Steffensmeier, Darrell; Feld, Barry C.; Morash, Merry; Chesney-Lind, Meda; Miller, Jody; Payne, Allison Ann; Gottfredson, Denise C.; & Kruttschnitt, Candace S. (2008) Violence by teenage girls: Trends and contexts. *Girls Study Group: Understanding and Responding to Girls' Delinquency* (Office of Juvenile Justice and Delinquency Prevention, U.S. Department of Justice, Washington, DC). At http://girlsstudygroup.rti.org/docs/OJJDP_GSG_Violence_Bulletin.pdf.

Index

About the Author

CINDY D. NESS is a practicing psychologist and adjunct professor at John Jay College of the City University of New York. She also is a Senior Policy Consultant at the Schuyler Center for Analysis and Advocacy in Albany.